GREAT TABASCO® RECIPES

BRIMAR

© 1996 Brimar Publishing Inc.
338 Saint Antoine St. East
Montreal, Canada H2Y 1A3
Tel. (514) 954-1441
Fax (514) 954-5806

Graphic Design: Zapp
Typesetting, Color Separation and Films: Caractéra
Photography: Rodrigo Gutierrez
Food Preparation/Stylist: Josée Robitaille
Assistant Stylist: Louis Hudon

Props courtesy of:
Arthur Quentin and Pier I Imports

Pictured on the front cover:
Paella (see recipe, page 82)

ISBN 2-89433-222-X
Printed in U.S.A.

TABASCO®
RECIPES

Today's cooks consider taste the most important attribute of any dish they serve. Tabasco® pepper sauce, produced by McIlhenny Company, Avery Island, Louisiana, has contributed superb flavor to the cuisines of the world for more than 125 years.

The clean, deep, distinctive character of Tabasco pepper sauce has long been acclaimed by chefs and home cooks around the globe. Now the famous brand appears on a line of sauces in the familiar narrow-necked bottles with the diamond-shaped logo and green neck bond. This includes two new sauces – milder Tabasco green jalapeño and Tabasco garlic pepper sauce blend – a gentler cayenne-based product.

These three sauces contribute their unique piquancy to the 135 kitchen-tested recipes offered in this cookbook. We hope you will enjoy these dishes and will use the Tabasco pepper sauces in your own favorite recipes, always remembering that even more can be added at the table!

How It Began

Avery Island, the birthplace of Tabasco® brand pepper sauce, is one of five salt dome "islands" rising above the flat bayou country of the U.S. Louisiana Gulf Coast. A salt brining industry on the Island dated back to about 1300 A.D., and a salt quarry begun in 1862 supplied Confederate troops fighting the war between the states, until Union forces took the Island and destroyed the salt works.

In the mid-1800s, New Orleans, strategically located on the Mississippi River, was one of the three largest cities in America. It was here that Edmund McIlhenny, a fifth generation American of Scottish-Irish descent, came from Hagerstown, Maryland in the 1840s. A banker by profession, he was also a bon vivant who enjoyed the good food and social life New Orleans offered.

In June of 1859, McIlhenny married Mary Eliza Avery whose family owned a sugar plantation on Isle Petit Anse, later to be called Avery Island. In 1862, the Averys left their home in Baton Rouge to oversee the salt-quarrying operation. A year later they were forced to flee from invading Union troops.

Before the war, McIlhenny, who loved to grow things, had planted in the Avery garden a special variety of red Capsicum peppers brought from Mexico by a friend. Surprisingly, the plants survived the devastation wrought by the Union troops. To add excitement to the monotonous food of the Reconstruction South, he experimented with making a pepper sauce, and hit upon a formula so popular with family and friends they encouraged him to sell it commercially.

Today, family-owned McIlhenny Company still makes Tabasco® pepper sauce in much the same way Edmund McIlhenny did in the 1860s. Carefully selected ripe red peppers are crushed immediately after harvest, mixed with Avery Island salt, aged in white oak barrels for up to three years, drained, blended with strong all natural vinegar, and stirred intermittently for weeks. The resulting sauce is strained, then bottled, capped and labelled.

Tabasco® sauce is now sold in over 100 countries around the world. It accompanied Carter on the excavation of King Tut's tomb, climbed to the top of Mt. Everest with Sir Edmund Hillary, was the subject of a debate in the British Parliament, journeyed into space with Skylab astronauts, and spiced up the rations of Desert Storm troops. As people discover its unique ability to enhance flavors, it becomes essential to their enjoyment of the foods they eat every day.

Recently, the original has been joined by two additional Tabasco® pepper sauces. Here are profiles of each:

TABASCO® Pepper Sauce: An all natural pure liquid red pepper sauce made from tabasco pepper mash combined with a small amount of salt, aged in white oak barrels for 3 years, then blended with strong high-quality vinegar. It is fat-free, low in sodium, and more concentrated than most pepper sauces. Available in 2-oz., 5-oz., 12-oz.. bottles and gallon jugs. Its unique flavor is delicious with eggs, sauces, gravies, cheese dishes, salad dressings, soups, meats, poultry, seafood, and even desserts. Use it in cooking, add a little more just before serving, and keep a bottle on the table.

TABASCO® Jalapeño Sauce: a sauce made from green jalapeño peppers mixed with vinegar and salt. Milder in flavor and lower on the heat scale, it delivers exceptional jalapeño taste without the bother of seeding, slicing or chopping peppers. Available in 2-oz. and 5-oz. bottles, it is excellent in all types of Mexican and southwestern foods, and enhances eggs, cheese dishes, seafood, chicken, beef, soups and salads.

TABASCO® Garlic Pepper Sauce Blend: A milder cayenne-based sauce enlivened with tabasco and red jalapeño peppers and garlic. Available in 5-oz. bottles, it provides a full-bodied garlic pepper flavor to everyday entrées as well as to marinades and sauces for chicken, fish and seafood, meat, pasta, pizza, and ethnic dishes.

The Tabasco® Country Store, located in the pepper sauce factory on Avery Island, used to be a tiny affair. But then visitors to the Island discovered its great red and green T-shirts, aprons, colorful neckties, boxer shorts, attractive gift items, housewares and regional specialty foods. It wasn't long before the store grew and branched out to cities like New Orleans and Tokyo. All of the unique items in the store, from gumbo bowls to a handsome wall clock, are available in the U.S. through a 22-page mail-order catalogue which may be obtained by calling 1-800-634-9599 (from the U.S. only) or writing McIlhenny Company, Avery Island, LA 70513.

Contents

◆ Eggs ◆

Fajitas and Eggs with Potatoes

A lively Mexican dish for brunch or supper.

1 tbsp	fresh lime juice	15 mL
1 tsp	Tabasco® pepper sauce	5 mL
1	clove garlic, minced	1
1 tsp	vegetable oil	5 mL
1 tsp	salt	5 mL
1/2 lb	beef skirt or flank steak	225 g
1	large russet potato, cooked, peeled and cut into 1/2-inch (1-cm) cubes	1
1/2 cup	chopped onion	125 mL
2 tbsp	chopped cilantro	30 mL
6	large eggs, lightly beaten	6
12	flour tortillas	12

◆ In a medium glass bowl, combine lime juice, Tabasco sauce, garlic, oil, and 1/2 tsp (2 mL) of salt; mix well.

◆ Slice steak diagonally against grain into 1/2-inch (1-cm) strips; cut strips into 1/2-inch (1-cm) cubes. Add beef to marinade and toss to coat. Cover with plastic wrap, and marinate at least 30 minutes at room temperature, turning occasionally.

◆ Cook steak until browned in a 12-inch (30-cm) non-stick skillet over medium-high heat; stir frequently. Add diced potatoes and reduce heat to medium. Cook, stirring constantly, 2 minutes or until potatoes are golden. Add onion and cook 2 minutes or until tender.

◆ Stir cilantro and remaining salt into eggs. Pour eggs into skillet. Cook about 3 minutes or until eggs are set, stirring constantly.

◆ Heat tortillas on a griddle or in a hot dry skillet, about 30 seconds on each side. Wrap in a kitchen towel to keep warm.

◆ Fill each tortilla with 1/3 cup (75 mL) cooked egg mixture. Wrap tortilla around filling and serve immediately with additional Tabasco pepper sauce, if desired.

(12 SERVINGS)

◆◆◆◆◆◆◆◆◆◆◆◆◆◆◆◆◆◆◆◆

Huevos Rancheros

A real breakfast warm-up.

2 tbsp	olive oil	30 mL
½ cup	chopped onion	125 mL
1	green pepper, chopped	1
1	tomato, peeled and chopped	1
1	clove garlic, minced	1
1 tsp	dried oregano	5 mL
½ tsp	salt	2 mL
1 tsp	Tabasco® pepper sauce	5 mL
1 cup	canned tomato sauce	250 mL
½ cup	water	125 mL
6	eggs	6
6	warm tortillas or toasted English muffin halves	6

◆ Heat olive oil in a large skillet over medium heat. Add onion and green pepper; cook until tender, about 5 minutes. Add tomato, garlic, oregano, salt, Tabasco sauce, tomato sauce and water. Cover and simmer 20 minutes over low heat.

◆ Break eggs, one at a time, into cup and slip into sauce. Cover and simmer over low heat about 5 minutes, or until eggs are set.

◆ Place eggs onto tortillas or toasted English muffin halves, top with sauce and serve.

(3 SERVINGS)

Poached Eggs à la Grecque

Whole olives, clove and nutmeg give these poached eggs a special flavor.

¹/₄ cup	**butter or margarine**	50 mL
¹/₄ cup	**thinly sliced onion**	50 mL
¹/₂ cup	**thinly sliced green pepper**	125 mL
¹/₂ cup	**sliced mushrooms**	125 mL
18	**small green olives**	18
3¹/₂ cups	**canned tomatoes in juice**	875 mL
¹/₂ tsp	**Tabasco® pepper sauce**	2 mL
1	**whole clove**	1
	Salt and pepper to taste	
6	**eggs**	6
	Nutmeg	

◆ Melt butter in a large shallow earthenware casserole or skillet. Add onions and peppers and sauté 2 to 3 minutes, or until vegetables are tender. Add mushrooms and olives and continue cooking 2 minutes, stirring occasionally. Add tomatoes, Tabasco sauce, clove, salt and pepper. Cover and simmer 20 minutes.

◆ Remove cover and carefully drop in eggs, one at a time. Allow eggs to poach until firm, about 5 or 6 minutes.

◆ Lightly dust the yolks with nutmeg and serve from the casserole or skillet.

(6 SERVINGS)

◆◆◆◆◆◆◆◆◆◆◆◆◆◆◆◆◆◆◆◆◆◆◆◆◆◆◆◆◆◆◆◆

Poached Eggs and Tomato with Spicy Mayonnaise

A lovely dish for brunch.

1/4 cup	mayonnaise	50 mL
1 tbsp	fresh chopped parsley	15 mL
1/2 tsp	Tabasco® pepper sauce	2 mL
1 tbsp	butter or margarine	15 mL
4	tomato slices	4
4	English muffins	4
2 tsp	vinegar	10 mL
4	large eggs	4

◆ In a small bowl, combine mayonnaise, parsley and Tabasco pepper sauce; set aside. Melt butter in a 10-inch (25-cm) skillet over medium heat; add tomato slices. Cook about 1 minute on each side, turning once. Toast English muffins.

◆ Fill a non-stick skillet 3/4 full with water; add vinegar. Bring to a boil over high heat; reduce heat to low. Break eggs, one at a time, into a saucer; slide each egg into the simmering water. Cook 3 minutes or until eggs are set.*

◆ Top each English muffin half with a tomato slice. With slotted spoon, carefully remove poached eggs from pan and place on tomato slices. Top with a dollop of Spicy Mayonnaise and serve with remaining English muffin halves on the side.

* *Eggs are done when whites become opaque and yolks lose their shine.*

(4 SERVINGS)

Scrambled Eggs Piperade

A wonderful dish for breakfast, brunch or supper.

1 tbsp	vegetable oil	15 mL
1	medium onion, cut in half and sliced	1
1/2	green bell pepper, seeded and sliced	1/2
1/2	red bell pepper, seeded and sliced	1/2
4	large eggs	4
1 tbsp	water	15 mL
1/2 tsp	salt	2 mL
1/2 tsp	Tabasco® pepper sauce	2 mL
1 tbsp	butter or margarine	15 mL
	Whole wheat toast	

◆ Heat oil in a 12-inch (30-cm) skillet over medium heat. Add onion and bell peppers. Cook, stirring occasionally, about 5 minutes, or until tender but firm.

◆ In a medium bowl, beat together eggs, water, salt and Tabasco sauce. Melt butter in a 10-inch (25-cm) non-stick skillet over medium heat; add egg mixture. Gently stir egg mixture, lifting it up and over the bottom as it thickens. Keep stirring to reach desired texture and consistency.

◆ Serve with pepper mixture and whole wheat toast.

(2 SERVINGS)

Classic Omelets

Tabasco sauce adds just the right note to eggs.

6	eggs	6
2 tbsp	water	30 mL
¼ tsp	salt	1 mL
½ tsp	Tabasco® pepper sauce	2 mL
3 tbsp	butter or margarine	45 mL
3 tbsp	grated Parmesan cheese – optional	45 mL

◆ In a mixing bowl, combine eggs with water, salt and Tabasco sauce. Beat until well-blended, but not frothy.

◆ Melt 1 tbsp (15 mL) of butter in an omelet pan over moderately high heat. Pour ⅓ of egg mixture into pan. Place left hand, palm downward, on pan handle and move pan back and forth. With right hand, stir eggs with fork in a circular motion, with flat part of fork touching bottom of pan without scraping.

◆ When omelet is cooked but still soft, reverse position of left hand so palm is upward. Sprinkle omelet with 1 tbsp (15 mL) of grated cheese, or desired filling. Tip pan and roll omelet out onto hot plate.

◆ Repeat with remaining egg mixture, butter and cheese for second and third omelets.

FILLINGS:

Bacon and Cheese: 1 slice cooked bacon, crumbled, and 1 tbsp (15 mL) grated Swiss cheese per omelet.

Seafood: 2 tbsp (30 mL) minced cooked lobster, crab or shrimp per omelette.

Fines Herbes: In a small bowl, combine 2 tbsp (30 mL) each of minced fresh parsley, tarragon and chives. Add to egg mixture before making omelets.

(3 SERVINGS)

◆ Appetizers ◆

Thai Pork and Pineapple

A wonderful, sweet and spicy appetizer.

2 tbsp	fish sauce	30 mL
4 tbsp	Tabasco® garlic pepper sauce blend	60 mL
2 tbsp	freshly squeezed lime juice	30 mL
2 tbsp	fresh cilantro, minced	30 mL
1	clove garlic, minced	1
1 tbsp	apricot preserves	15 mL
1½ lbs	pork shoulder, cut into l-inch (2.5-cm) cubes	675 g
2 tbsp	vegetable oil	30 mL
½ cup	brown sugar	125 mL
1	fresh pineapple, peeled, cored and cut into l-inch (2.5-cm) cubes	1
36	bamboo skewers	36

◆ In a medium bowl, mix fish sauce, 3 tbsp (45 mL) Tabasco garlic pepper sauce blend, lime juice, cilantro, garlic and apricot preserves. Add pork and marinate at least 4 hours in refrigerator.

◆ Heat oil in a wok or skillet over medium-high heat. Meanwhile, drain pork cubes and reserve marinade. Stir-fry pork in hot oil, in batches if necessary, being sure to sear the meat well.

◆ Add marinade to wok and stir. Gradually incorporate brown sugar and remaining Tabasco garlic pepper sauce blend, stirring after each addition. Continue stirring until mixture has a syrup-like consistency. Remove from heat.

◆ Alternate pieces of pork and pineapple on skewers. Arrange on serving platter and serve at room temperature.

(36 SKEWERS)

◆◆◆◆◆◆◆◆◆◆◆◆◆◆◆◆◆◆◆◆◆◆◆

Chicken in Phyllo Packets

A delightful hot appetizer from the Orient.

½ lb	boneless, skinless chicken breast, cut into strips	225 g
3 tbsp	Tabasco® garlic pepper sauce blend	45 mL
1 tbsp	hoisin sauce	15 mL
1 tsp	soy sauce	5 mL
1 tsp	sesame oil	5 mL
2 tsp	cornstarch	10 mL
1 tbsp	fresh cilantro, minced	15 mL
1	garlic clove, chopped	1
¼ lb	butter	125 g
1 tbsp	Tabasco® pepper sauce	15 mL
8	phyllo sheets (12 × 17-inch or 30 × 43-cm)	8
	Black sesame seeds for garnishing	

◆ In a medium bowl, combine chicken strips, Tabasco garlic pepper sauce blend, hoisin sauce, soy sauce, sesame oil, cornstarch, cilantro and garlic. Cover and let stand at least 15 minutes.*

◆ Preheat oven to 425°F (220°C).

◆ Melt butter with Tabasco pepper sauce in a small saucepan over medium heat.

◆ Cut phyllo sheets in half to make two 12 × 8½-inch (30 × 21-cm) sheets. Butter one side of each sheet with Tabasco sauce/butter mixture and fold over again to make 12 × 4¼-inch (30 × 10.5-cm) sheets. Cut folded sheet in half to make two equal pieces, 6 × 4¼-inch (15 × 10.5-cm).

◆ Spoon 1 tsp (5 mL) of chicken mixture onto each piece. Fold over twice and then wrap sides around chicken and seal with a little butter to form a rectangular package approximately 2 × 1-inch (5 × 2.5-cm). Repeat with remaining phyllo sheets and chicken mixture.

◆ Place chicken packets on baking sheet. Brush with remaining Tabasco sauce/butter mixture and sprinkle with sesame seeds.

◆ Bake 10 to 15 minutes, or until lightly golden. Serve warm.

* *The chicken filling can be prepared one day ahead and refrigerated.*

(32 APPETIZER PIECES)

Butter one side of each phyllo sheet with Tabasco sauce/butter mixture.

Fold phyllo again to make 12 × 4¼-inch (30 × 10.5-cm) sheets.

Cut folded sheet in half to make two equal pieces, 6 × 4¼-inch (15 × 10.5-cm).

Spoon 1 tsp (5 mL) of chicken mixture onto each piece.

Fold over twice and then wrap sides around chicken.

Seal with a little butter to form a rectangular package approximately 2 × 1-inch (5 × 2.5-cm).

Mussels Vinaigrette

These mussels with their colorful vinaigrette dressing make marvellous hors d'œuvres or a light lunch.

24	mussels	24
1 cup	water	250 mL
3	lemon slices	3
3 tbsp	red wine vinegar	45 mL
2 tbsp	olive oil	30 mL
2 tbsp	finely chopped red pepper	30 mL
2 tbsp	finely chopped onion	30 mL
2 tbsp	finely chopped parsley	30 mL
1	large garlic clove, minced	1
1/4 tsp	salt	1 mL
1/2 tsp	Tabasco® pepper sauce	2 mL

◆ Scrub mussels well, discarding any that are not tightly closed.

◆ Put water and lemon slices in a large saucepan; add mussels and bring to a boil. Simmer over low heat 3 to 5 minutes or until mussels open. Remove pan and let cool mussels and reserved liquid. Discard any mussels that have not opened.

◆ Meanwhile, combine remaining ingredients in a medium bowl.

◆ Remove mussels from shells, reserving half of shells. Add 1/3 cup (75 mL) cooled liquid and mussels to vegetable mixture; mix well. Cover and refrigerate at least 2 hours, stirring occasionally.

◆ Place mussels in shells, top with small amount of marinade, and serve.

(4 SERVINGS)

Peruvian Ceviche

Delicate fish slices "cooked" in lime juice.

2 lbs	striped bass, thinly sliced	900 g	1	Spanish onion, very thinly sliced	1
¹/₂ cup	lime juice	125 mL	2	green onions, finely chopped	2
1 tsp	salt	5 mL			
¹/₄ tsp	Tabasco® pepper sauce	1 mL	¹/₂	pimiento pepper, finely chopped	¹/₂
¹/₂ cup	grapefruit juice	125 mL	¹/₂	green pepper, finely chopped	¹/₂
1¹/₂ tbsp	minced onion	25 mL			
1¹/₂ tbsp	minced green pepper	25 mL	2 tbsp	cooked corn kernels	30 mL
1 tsp	chopped fresh chives or cilantro	5 mL	2	grapefruit, in sections	2

◆ Place raw bass slices in a bowl with lime juice, salt and Tabasco pepper sauce. Toss to coat bass well. Marinate 12 hours or overnight. Add grapefruit juice, onion, green pepper and chives or cilantro.

◆ Arrange bass on deep platter; pour marinade over it and top with Spanish onion slices. Scatter green onions, pimiento, chopped green pepper and corn kernels over the fish. Garnish with fresh grapefruit sections and serve.

(8 SERVINGS)

◆ ◆

Jalapeño Almonds

Spicy nibbles for cool drinks.

1/4 cup	salted butter or margarine	50 mL
1/3 cup	Tabasco® jalapeño sauce	75 mL
1 tbsp	Tabasco® pepper sauce	15 mL
1 tbsp	Worcestershire sauce	15 mL
1 1/2 tsp	garlic powder	7 mL
1 1/2 tsp	salt	7 mL
1 tsp	dry mustard	5 mL
1 lb	whole almonds	450 g

◆ Preheat oven to 325°F (160°C).

◆ Melt butter in a small saucepan over low heat; stir in all sauces, garlic powder, salt and mustard. Remove to a large roasting pan and incorporate almonds.

◆ Bake 1 hour, stirring occasionally. Let almonds cool completely and serve.

(1 lb – 450 g)

Jalapeñorita

A margarita with a whole new zip.

1 1/4 oz	gold tequila	35 mL
2/3 oz	Grand Marnier	20 mL
	Juice of 1/2 a lime	
1/2 tsp	Tabasco® jalapeño sauce	2 mL

◆ Rub the rim of a goblet with the cut side of a lime, then dip rim into a saucer of salt. Fill glass with ice. Pour first 3 ingredients into an ice-filled cocktail shaker, and shake vigorously.

◆ Strain into ice-filled glass. Stir in Tabasco jalapeño sauce and garnish with a slice of lime.

VARIATION: Use margarita or sweet-and-sour mix and make the drink as directed on the label. Stir in 1/2 to 1 tsp (2 mL to 5 mL) jalapeño sauce per drink.

(1 DRINK)

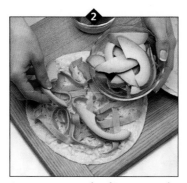

Cut slices of ham into ¹/₂-inch (1-cm) strips and place over cheese.

Arrange avocado slices over the ham.

Top ham and cheese with chopped tomato.

◆ ◆

Sincronizadas

A wonderful snack, cut into wedges.

2 tbsp	Tabasco® jalapeño sauce	30 mL
12	flour tortillas	12
2 cups	shredded Monterey Jack cheese	500 mL
6	thin slices of ham, cut into ¹/₂-inch (1-cm) strips	6
2	ripe avocados, peeled, pitted and sliced	2
¹/₃ cup	chopped tomato	75 mL
¹/₄ cup	chopped cilantro	50 mL

◆ Place six tortillas on flat surface. Spread about ¹/₂ tsp (2 mL) of Tabasco jalapeño sauce on each.

◆ Distribute half of cheese over tortillas. Layer on ham strips, avocado slices, chopped tomato, cilantro and remaining cheese.

◆ Spread one side of remaining six tortillas with remaining jalapeño sauce and place sauce sidedown on layered tortillas, forming sandwiches (sincronizades).

◆ On a griddle or in a medium-size skillet, cook sincronizadas one at a time over medium heat, until tortillas are crisp and lightly browned on each side, and cheese is melted. Remove to a platter, cut into wedges and serve with additional Tabasco jalapeño sauce, if desired.

(6 SERVINGS)

Sprinkle cilantro over tortillas.

Distribute remaining cheese over cilantro.

Top with another tortilla, sauce side down, forming a tortilla sandwich (sincronizada).

Chicken, Beef and Vegetable Kebabs

Colorful party brighteners.

1 cup	fresh pearl onions	250 mL
1 tbsp	Tabasco® pepper sauce	15 mL
1/3 cup	olive oil	75 mL
2 tbsp	balsamic vinegar	30 mL
1 tbsp	dried basil	15 mL
2	large cloves garlic, crushed	2
1 tsp	salt	5 mL
1 lb	boneless, skinless chicken breast	450 g
1 lb	boneless beef sirloin	450 g
2	large red peppers, cored, seeded and cut into 3/4-inch (2-cm) pieces	2
1	large green pepper, cored, seeded and cut into 3/4-inch (2-cm) pieces	1
1	large zucchini, cut into 3/4-inch (2-cm) pieces	1

◆ Soak 3 dozen short wooden skewers in water overnight.

◆ Place pearl onions in a 1-qt (1-L) saucepan and cover with water. Bring to a boil over high heat. Reduce heat to low. Cover and simmer 3 minutes or until onions are tender; drain. When cool enough to handle, peel away the outer layer of skin.

◆ In a medium bowl, combine Tabasco pepper sauce, oil, balsamic vinegar, basil, garlic and salt. Pour half of the mixture into another bowl.

◆ Cut chicken and beef into 3/4-inch (2-cm) chunks and place them in one of the bowls; toss well to coat. In the remaining bowl of Tabasco pepper sauce mixture, toss cooked pearl onions, peppers and zucchini. Let stand at least 30 minutes, stirring occasionally.

◆ Preheat broiler. Skewer one chunk of chicken or beef and one each of red pepper, green pepper, onion and zucchini onto each wooden pick. Broil 4 to 6 minutes, turning occasionally, and serve.

(3 DOZEN HORS D'ŒUVRES)

Chicken Jalapeño Spread

A hot hors d'œuvre to shout about.

2	boneless, skinless chicken breast halves	2
1 tbsp	olive oil	15 mL
8 oz	cream cheese, softened	240 g
¼ cup	mayonnaise	50 mL
¼ cup	milk	50 mL
¼ cup	minced red bell pepper	50 mL
2 tbsp	minced jalapeño pepper	30 mL
1 tbsp	lemon juice	15 mL
¾ tsp	salt	3 mL
¾ tsp	Tabasco® pepper sauce	3 mL

◆ Preheat oven to 375°F (190°C).

◆ Finely chop chicken breast. Heat oil in a 12-inch (30-cm) skillet over medium-high heat. Cook chicken, stirring frequently, until tender and golden on all sides.

◆ In a medium bowl, combine remaining ingredients and cooked chicken until well blended.

◆ Spoon chicken mixture into an ovenproof crock or small casserole. Bake 20 minutes or until mixture is hot and bubbly. Serve with crisp crackers or pita triangles.

(3 CUPS – 750 ML)

◆◆◆◆◆◆◆◆◆◆◆◆◆◆◆◆◆◆◆◆◆◆◆

Spicy Chicken Wings
with Creamy Jalapeño Sauce

An exciting variation on an American favorite.

8	**large chicken wings**	8
¼ cup	**Tabasco® jalapeño sauce**	50 mL
¼ cup	**Worcestershire sauce**	50 mL

CREAMY JALAPEÑO SAUCE

½ cup	**light sour cream**	125 mL
¼ cup	**Tabasco® jalapeño sauce**	50 mL
¼ cup	**fresh chopped parsley**	50 mL
1 tbsp	**white wine Worcestershire sauce**	15 mL

◆ Cut chicken wings at joint; discard wing tips. In a medium bowl, combine Tabasco jalapeño sauce and Worcestershire sauce; add chicken pieces. Cover and let marinate at least 4 hours.

◆ Preheat oven to 400°F (200°C). Arrange chicken on a large baking sheet. Cook 30 to 40 minutes or until chicken is tender, brushing with sauce and turning occasionally. Serve with Creamy Jalapeño Sauce.

◆ In a small bowl, combine all ingredients and stir until smooth. Serve with Spicy Chicken Wings.

(4 SERVINGS)

◆◆◆◆◆◆◆◆◆◆◆◆◆◆◆◆◆◆◆◆◆◆◆◆◆◆◆

Baked Oysters Casino

This is delicious with fresh clams, too.

3	bacon slices, chopped	3
1/4 cup	chopped onion	50 mL
1/4 cup	chopped green pepper	50 mL
2 tbsp	chopped celery	30 mL
1 tsp	lemon juice	5 mL
1/2 tsp	salt	2 mL
1/2 tsp	Tabasco® pepper sauce	2 mL
1/2 tsp	Worcestershire sauce	2 mL
36	oysters, drained	36
	Lemon slices and parsley sprigs	

◆ Preheat oven to 400°F (200°C).

◆ Cook bacon in a 10-inch (25-cm) skillet over medium heat until crisp. Add onion, green pepper and celery; cook until tender, about 5 minutes. Stir in remaining ingredients, except oysters.

◆ Open oysters and place in shallow buttered baking dish. Spread bacon mixture over oysters. Bake in oven 10 minutes, or until edges of oysters begin to curl.

◆ Garnish with lemon slices and sprigs of parsley; serve.

(6 SERVINGS)

Bloody Mary Pitcher

Without Tabasco pepper sauce, the Bloody Mary would be a dull drink.

1 qt	thick tomato juice	1 L
1 1/2 cups	vodka or gin	375 mL
4 tsp	fresh lime or lemon juice	20 mL
1 tbsp	Worcestershire sauce	15 mL
1 tsp	salt	5 mL
1/4 tsp	Tabasco® pepper sauce	1 mL
	Lime slices or celery stalks	

◆ Combine all ingredients in a 2-qt (2-L) pitcher. Stir well and refrigerate until chilled.

◆ When ready to serve, stir again and pour into tall ice-filled glasses. Garnish with slices of lime or celery stalks. For an even spicier drink, add more Tabasco pepper sauce.

(8 DRINKS)

♦ Breads ♦

◆ ◆

Cheddar Jalapeño Bread

Exciting, spicy, cheesy flavor.

2	envelopes active dry yeast	2
1 tsp	granulated sugar	5 mL
1/2 cup	warm water (110°F – 50°C)	125 mL
83/4 cups	all-purpose flour	2 L, 175 mL
3 cups	shredded extra-sharp cheddar cheese	750 mL
1/4 cup	minced jalapeño pepper	50 mL
1 tbsp	salt	15 mL
2 tsp	Tabasco® pepper sauce	10 mL
2 cups	milk	500 mL
4	large eggs	4

◆ In a small bowl, combine yeast, sugar and warm water. Let stand 5 minutes until foamy.

◆ In a large bowl, combine 8 cups (2 L) flour, cheddar cheese, jalapeño pepper, salt and Tabasco pepper sauce.

◆ Warm milk in a small saucepan over low heat; add yeast mixture. Stir milk into flour mixture.

◆ In a medium bowl, lightly beat eggs. Set aside 1 tbsp (15 mL) beaten egg to brush on dough later. Add remaining eggs to flour mixture; stir until mixture makes a soft dough.

◆ On a lightly floured surface, knead dough 5 minutes or until smooth and elastic, incorporating the remaining 3/4 cup (175 mL) flour. Shape dough into a ball and place in a large, greased bowl, turning dough over to grease the top. Cover with a towel and let rise in a warm place until doubled, about 11/2 hours.

◆ Grease two large cookie sheets. Punch down dough and divide in half. Shape each half of dough into a ball and place balls on cookie sheets. Cover with a towel and let rise in a warm place until doubled, about 11/2 hours.

◆ Preheat oven to 375°F (190°C). Brush loaves with reserved beaten egg. Bake loaves about 45 minutes or until loaves sound hollow when lightly tapped. Remove to wire racks to cool.

(2 LOAVES)

◆◆◆◆◆◆◆◆◆◆◆◆◆◆◆◆◆◆◆◆◆◆◆

Cheddar Cheese Biscuits

These zesty cheese biscuits, piping hot from the oven,
are especially good with soups and salads.

2 cups	sifted all-purpose flour	500 mL
1 tbsp	baking powder	15 mL
1 tsp	salt	5 mL
1/2 cup	grated sharp cheddar cheese	125 mL
6 tbsp	shortening	90 mL
1 1/2 tsp	Tabasco® pepper sauce	7 mL
2/3 cup	milk	150 mL

◆ Preheat oven to 400°F (200°C).

◆ In a mixing bowl, sift together flour, baking powder and salt. Stir in grated cheese. Cut in shortening, using pastry blender or two knives.*

◆ Stir Tabasco pepper sauce into milk; add to flour mixture, blending lightly and quickly. If dough is not moist enough to stick together, add a few more drops of milk.

◆ Turn onto lightly floured board or pastry cloth. Lightly knead 6 to 7 times. Roll until 1/2-inch (1-cm) thick. Cut with floured 2-inch (5-cm) biscuit cutter. Bake on ungreased baking sheet 12 to 15 minutes.

* *A shortcut method is to put dry ingredients, cheese and shortening into the bowl of a food processor and process until mixture looks like coarse bread crumbs.*

(1 1/2 DOZEN)

Mushroom and Sun-Dried Tomato Pizza

A green salad and a glass of wine would complete this simple supper.

1½ oz	sun-dried tomatoes, cut into ¼-inch (0.5 cm) slices	45 g
1¾ cups	canned diced tomatoes	425 mL
2 cups	sliced fresh mushrooms	500 mL
2 tbsp	chopped fresh basil, or ½ tsp (2 mL) dried basil	30 mL
2 tbsp	chopped fresh parsley	30 mL
2 tsp	Tabasco® garlic pepper sauce blend	10 mL
¼ tsp	salt	1 mL
1	10-oz (300 g) can refrigerated pizza crust	1
1	small zucchini, thinly sliced (optional)	1
1 cup	shredded mozzarella cheese	250 mL

◆ Combine sun-dried tomatoes and ½ cup (125 mL) of water in a saucepan; set aside 15 minutes. Add canned tomatoes and bring to a boil; reduce heat and simmer 15 minutes.

◆ Add next 5 ingredients and cook 5 minutes longer or until liquid has evaporated, stirring frequently.

◆ Preheat oven to 425°F (220°C). Press pizza dough out onto greased 12-inch (30-cm) pizza pan and spread on tomato mixture; if desired, arrange zucchini slices on top. Sprinkle with cheese and bake 12 to 15 minutes or until crust is golden brown.

(6 SERVINGS)

◆◆◆◆◆◆◆◆◆◆◆◆◆◆◆◆◆◆◆◆◆◆◆◆◆◆◆

Pepper Baguettes

Crisp-crusted loaves with a peppery zing.

1 cup	lukewarm water	250 mL
1	envelope active dry yeast	1
1 tbsp	Tabasco® pepper sauce	15 mL
1 tsp	granulated sugar	5 mL
2½ cups	unbleached flour	625 mL
½ tsp	salt	2 mL
1 tbsp	cornmeal	15 mL

◆ Place water in food processor and sprinkle in yeast, Tabasco pepper sauce and sugar. Set aside 5 minutes. Lightly oil a 4 to 5-quart (4 to 5-L) bowl.

◆ Add flour and salt to yeast mixture in food processor and blend 30 seconds to 1 minute, or until dough leaves side of bowl. Transfer dough to oiled bowl. Cover and allow to rise at room temperature 1 to 1½ hours, or until dough has doubled in size.

◆ When dough has doubled, punch it down and form into a ball. Place it on a lightly floured surface and divide it into 3 parts. Lightly grease a baking sheet and sprinkle it with corn meal.

◆ Shape dough into three baguettes and place on baking sheet. Cover with plastic wrap and allow bread to rise 40 minutes.

◆ Preheat oven to 400°F (200°C). While oven is heating, place a small ovenproof pan beneath rack to be used for the bread.

◆ After second rise, sprinkle baguettes with flour and slash tops with a sharp knife. Place baking sheet in oven, then fill the hot pan underneath ¾ full with ice cubes. Ice will melt and create steam to crisp crust. Bake 30 minutes or until golden. Remove and cool on a rack.

(3 BAGUETTES)

Place water in food processor and sprinkle in yeast, Tabasco pepper sauce and sugar.

Add flour and salt to food processor and blend until dough leaves side of bowl.

Transfer dough to oiled bowl. Cover and allow to rise at room temperature until dough has doubled in size.

Lightly grease a baking sheet and sprinkle it with corn meal.

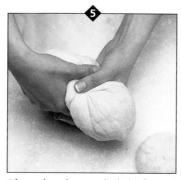

Place dough on a lightly floured surface and divide it into 3 parts.

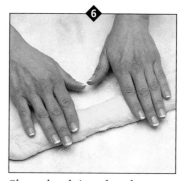

Shape dough into three baguettes and place on baking sheet.

◆◆◆◆◆◆◆◆◆◆◆◆◆◆◆◆◆◆◆◆◆◆◆◆◆◆◆

Southwestern Pizza

A spicy version of an Italian favorite.

DOUGH:

1	**envelope active dry yeast**	1
3/4 cup	**warm water** **(110°F – 55°C)**	175 mL
2 cups	**all-purpose flour**	500 mL
1 tsp	**salt**	5 mL
	Yellow cornmeal	

TOPPING:

2 cups	**shredded** **Monterey Jack cheese**	500 mL
1 cup	**sliced Chorizo sausage**	250 mL
1	**plum tomato, sliced**	1
3 tbsp	**chopped green chilies**	45 mL
2	**green onions, sliced**	2
1/2 cup	**sliced black olives**	125 mL
1 tsp	**Tabasco® pepper sauce**	5 mL

◆ Sprinkle yeast over water in a small bowl; stir to dissolve yeast. Let stand about 5 minutes. Stir in flour and salt to make a soft dough.

◆ Turn dough onto lightly floured surface. Knead until smooth and elastic, about 5 minutes, adding more flour if necessary. Shape into a ball. Place in a greased bowl; turn to coat. Cover and let rise in warm place until doubled, about 1 hour.

◆ Preheat oven to 425°F (220°C). Sprinkle a large baking sheet or jelly-roll pan with cornmeal. Punch down dough. Roll or pat dough into a 13 × 9-inch (32 × 22-cm) rectangle.

◆ Cover crust with 1/2 of cheese and other topping ingredients. Sprinkle remaining cheese on top.

◆ Bake on lowest rack 20 minutes or until crust is golden brown.

(6 SERVINGS)

◆ 36 ◆

Shamrock Scones

Delicious flavor, fun shape.

3½ cups	all-purpose flour	875 mL
5 tsp	baking powder	25 mL
1 tsp	salt	5 mL
¾ cup	butter or margarine	175 mL
4	large eggs	4
½ cup	milk	125 mL
2 tbsp	Tabasco® jalapeño sauce	30 mL
⅓ cup	minced green onions	75 mL

◆ Preheat oven to 425°F (220°C). In a large bowl, combine flour, baking powder and salt. With pastry blender or two knives, cut in butter until mixture resembles coarse crumbs.

◆ In a medium bowl, beat eggs, milk and Tabasco jalapeño sauce. Incorporate milk mixture to dry ingredients; stir in green onions.

◆ On lightly-floured surface with lightly-floured hands, pat dough until ½-inch (1-cm) thick. Cut dough with 3-inch (7-cm) shamrock or round cookie cutter. Reuse scraps.

◆ Place scones on lightly greased cookie sheet. Bake 12 minutes or until golden. Remove to cooling rack. Serve warm or let cool completely.

(12 SERVINGS)

Roll or pat dough into a 13 × 9-inch (32 × 22-cm) rectangle.

Spoon onions over dough.

Top with roasted red pepper strips, rosemary, Tabasco pepper sauce and salt.

Sweet Onion Focaccia

Fun to make; heaven to eat.

DOUGH:

1	**envelope active dry yeast**	1
³/4 cup	**warm water (110°F – 55°C)**	175 mL
2 cups	**all-purpose flour**	500 mL
1 tsp	**salt**	5 mL
	Yellow cornmeal	

TOPPING:

2 tbsp	**olive oil**	30 mL
1	**large red onion, sliced**	1
1	**large yellow onion, sliced**	1
1	**7-oz (210 g) jar roasted red peppers, drained and sliced**	1
2 tsp	**fresh chopped rosemary or ³/4 tsp (3 mL) dried rosemary**	10 mL
¹/2 tsp	**Tabasco® pepper sauce**	2 mL
¹/8 tsp	**salt**	0.5 mL

◆ Sprinkle yeast over water in small bowl; stir to dissolve yeast and let stand about 5 minutes. Stir in flour and salt to make a soft dough.

◆ Turn dough onto lightly floured surface. Knead until smooth and elastic, about 5 minutes, adding more flour if necessary. Shape into a ball and place in a greased bowl; turn to coat. Cover and let rise in warm place until doubled, about 1 hour.

◆ While crust is rising, heat oil in a 12-inch (30-cm) skillet over medium-high heat. Add onions and cook until tender, about 8 minutes, stirring occasionally.

◆ Preheat oven to 425°F (220°C). Sprinkle a large baking sheet or jelly-roll pan with cornmeal. Punch down dough. Roll or pat dough into a 13 × 9-inch (32 × 22-cm) rectangle. Place on baking sheet.

◆ Spoon onions over dough; top with roasted red pepper strips, rosemary, Tabasco pepper sauce and salt. Bake on lowest rack 20 minutes or until crust is golden brown.

(6 SERVINGS)

◆ Soups ◆

◆◆◆◆◆◆◆◆◆◆◆◆◆◆◆◆◆◆◆◆◆◆◆◆

Spicy Bean Soup

Bacon, garlic and cilantro enhance this hearty soup.

1 cup	dried pinto beans, washed	250 mL
5 cups	cold water	1.2 L
1/2 tsp	salt	2 mL
2	bacon slices, diced	2
1/2 cup	chopped onion	125 mL
1	clove garlic, minced	1
1	large tomato, peeled, seeded and chopped	1
3 1/2 cups	chicken broth	875 mL
1 tsp	Tabasco® pepper sauce	5 mL
2 tbsp	uncooked elbow macaroni	30 mL
1/4 cup	chopped cilantro	50 mL

◆ In a 6-qt (6-L) heavy deep kettle or saucepan, place beans with enough hot water to cover by 2 inches (5 cm). Let stand at least 1 hour.

◆ Drain beans and rinse. Add 5 cups (1.2 L) cold water. Heat to boiling; lower heat. Cover and simmer 2 hours, or until beans are tender, stirring occasionally. Add salt 15 minutes before beans are cooked.

◆ With a blender or food processor, combine 1 cup (250 mL) cooked beans with 1 cup (250 mL) of their cooking liquid. Process until smooth and set aside.

◆ Cook bacon in a skillet over medium heat until crisp. Drain all except 2 tsp (10 mL) of bacon drippings. Add onion and garlic to skillet; cook until tender. Add tomato, cook 1 minute.

◆ Transfer bacon mixture to original saucepan with remaining beans. Add chicken broth, blended beans and Tabasco pepper sauce. Bring to a boil and add macaroni. Lower heat and cook until macaroni is tender, approximately 7 minutes.

◆ When macaroni is cooked, add cilantro and adjust seasonings with salt and additional Tabasco pepper sauce, if desired. Serve immediately.

(8 SERVINGS)

◆◆◆◆◆◆◆◆◆◆◆◆◆◆◆◆◆◆◆◆◆◆◆◆◆◆◆

Chicken Tortilla Soup

A blend of tantalizing Mexican flavors.

2	**large ripe avocados, halved and pitted**	2
1/2 tsp	**salt**	2 mL
4 tsp	**Tabasco® jalapeño sauce, divided**	20 mL
6 cups	**chicken broth**	1.5 L
3	**skinless, boneless chicken breast halves**	3
2 tbsp	**uncooked rice**	30 mL
1	**large tomato, seeded and chopped**	1
1/2 cup	**chopped onion**	125 mL
1/4 cup	**finely chopped cilantro**	50 mL
	Tortilla chips	
1/2 cup	**shredded Monterey Jack cheese**	125 mL

◆ Scoop avocados into a medium bowl and mash with a fork; add salt and 1½ tsp (7 mL) Tabasco jalapeño sauce. Blend gently but thoroughly. Set aside.

◆ In a 4-qt (4-L) saucepan, bring chicken broth to a boil. Add chicken breasts, lower heat, and cook until white throughout. Remove chicken and cut into bite-size pieces. Add rice to broth and cook until tender, approximately 15 minutes. Return chicken to saucepan.

◆ Add tomato, onion, cilantro and remaining 2½ tsp (12 mL) Tabasco jalapeño sauce. Break a small handful of tortilla chips into each bowl. Ladle soup over tortilla chips. Top with 1 tbsp (15 mL) cheese and 1 tbsp (15 mL) avocado mixture. Serve immediately with additional Tabasco jalapeño sauce, if desired.

(8 SERVINGS)

◆◆◆◆◆◆◆◆◆◆◆◆◆◆◆◆◆◆◆◆◆◆◆◆◆

Corn and Chicken Chowder

Perfect for lunch or supper.

3 tbsp	butter or margarine	45 mL
1 lb	chicken breasts, cut into chunks	450 g
2	medium leeks, sliced	2
2	medium potatoes, cut into bite-size chunks	2
1	large green pepper, diced	1
2 tbsp	paprika	30 mL
2 tbsp	all-purpose flour	30 mL
3 cups	chicken broth	750 mL
2½ cups	fresh or canned corn kernels	625 mL
1½ tsp	Tabasco® pepper sauce	7 mL
1 tsp	salt	5 mL
1 cup	half-and-half cream	250 mL

◆ Melt 1 tbsp (15 mL) of butter in a 4-qt (4-L) saucepan over medium-high heat. Add chicken and cook until well-browned on all sides, stirring frequently. With slotted spoon, remove chicken to plate.

◆ Add remaining butter to drippings in saucepan. Over medium heat, cook leeks, potatoes and green pepper until tender, stirring occasionally. Stir in paprika and flour until well-blended; cook 1 minute.

◆ Add chicken broth, corn kernels, Tabasco pepper sauce, salt and chicken chunks. Bring to a boil over high heat. Reduce heat to low; cover and simmer 20 minutes. Stir in cream, heat through and serve.

(8 SERVINGS)

Oyster Rockefeller Soup

A souped-up Louisiana classic.

2¹/₂ tbsp	butter or margarine	40 mL
5 tbsp	all-purpose flour	75 mL
2	cloves garlic, minced	2
1	bunch green onions (tops only)	1
20 oz	oysters, minced	600 g
1³/₄ cups	canned reduced salt chicken broth	425 mL
1¹/₂ cups	skim milk	375 mL
1¹/₂ cups	canned evaporated skim milk	375 mL
2	10-oz (300-g) packages frozen chopped spinach, thawed and squeezed dry	2
¹/₂ tsp	Tabasco® pepper sauce	2 mL
	Salt to taste	

◆ Melt butter or margarine in large soup pot and stir in flour. Add garlic and onions; cook over medium high heat until onions are transparent.

◆ Add oysters and cook until firm. Add chicken broth, milk and evaporated milk; stir well to combine. Add spinach and bring to a boil.

◆ Remove from heat and allow to cool slightly. Process in a blender or food processor until well-blended. Season with Tabasco pepper sauce and salt, if desired.

(4 SERVINGS)

◆ ◆

Chicken and Sweet Sausage Gumbo

For full flavor, don't hurry this dish.

4 tbsp	vegetable oil, divided	60 mL
1	10-oz (300-g) package frozen okra, thawed and thinly sliced crosswise	1
1 lb	sweet sausage, sliced into 1-inch (2.5-cm) pieces	450 g
1	3-lb (1.4-kg) chicken, cut into 8 pieces	1
1/3 cup	all-purpose flour	75 mL
1 cup	*each* chopped onion, green pepper and green onions	250 mL
1/2 cup	chopped celery	125 mL
2 tbsp	minced parsley	30 mL
2	cloves garlic, minced	2
2 cups	canned whole tomatoes	500 mL
2 tbsp	tomato paste	30 mL
1 1/2 qts	water	1.5 L
2	bay leaves	2
1 tbsp	Worcestershire sauce	15 mL
1 tsp	thyme, crumbled	5 mL
1 tsp	salt	5 mL
1 1/4 tsp	Tabasco® pepper sauce	6 mL
	Hot steamed rice	
	Chopped green onion or parsley	

◆ Heat 2 tbsp (30 mL) of oil in a large stock pot or kettle. Add sliced okra and cook, stirring constantly, 10 to 15 minutes, or until tender and lightly browned. Remove from pot and set aside.

◆ In same pot, heat 1 tbsp (15 mL) of oil and brown sausages; remove and set aside. Add chicken and brown on all sides; remove and set aside.

◆ Measure fat remaining in pot. If necessary add vegetable oil to make 3 tbsp (45 mL). Stir in flour and cook over medium heat, stirring constantly until mixture turns a dark brown and develops a nutty flavor, about 20 minutes.

◆ Add onion, bell pepper, green onion, celery, parsley and garlic; cook until vegetables are tender. Add tomatoes, tomato paste, okra, water, bay leaves, Worcestershire sauce, thyme, salt and Tabasco pepper sauce. Simmer, uncovered, 15 minutes.

◆ Add chicken and sausage; cover and simmer 40 minutes, or until chicken is tender.

◆ Serve over steamed rice with additional Tabasco pepper sauce, if desired. Garnish with chopped green onion or parsley.

(8 SERVINGS)

Add sliced okra to stock pot and cook, stirring constantly, 10 to 15 minutes.

In same pot, heat 1 tbsp (15 mL) of oil and brown sausages; remove and set aside.

Add chicken to stock pot and brown on all sides; remove and set aside.

Add onion, bell pepper, green onion, celery, parsley and garlic; cook until vegetables are tender.

Add tomatoes, tomato paste, okra, water, bay leaves, Worcestershire sauce, thyme, salt and Tabasco pepper sauce. Simmer, uncovered, 15 minutes.

Add chicken and sausage; cover and simmer 40 minutes, or until chicken is tender.

◆◆◆◆◆◆◆◆◆◆◆◆◆◆◆◆◆◆◆◆◆◆◆◆

Carrot Vichyssoise

A cool tangy soup; also delicious served hot.

1 1/2 cups	pared, sliced potatoes	375 mL
1/2 cup	pared, sliced carrots	125 mL
1/2 cup	thinly sliced leeks (white part only)	125 mL
2 cups	chicken broth	500 mL
1/8 tsp	salt	0.5 mL
1 cup	milk	250 mL
1/2 tsp	Tabasco® pepper sauce	2 mL

◆ In a medium size saucepan, combine potatoes, carrots, leeks, chicken broth and salt. Bring to a boil. Reduce heat, cover and cook until very tender, 40 to 45 minutes.

◆ Process with electric blender or food processor until smooth. Add milk and Tabasco pepper sauce; mix well. Chill and serve cold or reheat and serve hot. Garnish with carrot curls or grated carrot and parsley.

(4 SERVINGS)

Chilled Zucchini Soup

A cool starter for summer meals.

3 1/2 cups	low-sodium chicken broth	875 mL
5	medium zucchini, sliced	5
1	large onion, chopped	1
1	clove garlic, chopped	1
3 tbsp	fresh basil, chopped	45 mL
1/2 tsp	salt	2 mL
1/2 tsp	Tabasco® pepper sauce	2 mL
2 tsp	cornstarch	10 mL
1 cup	low-fat plain yogurt	250 mL

◆ In a large saucepan, combine chicken broth, zucchini, onion, garlic, basil, salt and Tabasco pepper sauce. Bring to a boil, reduce heat, and simmer 15 minutes or until vegetables are tender.

◆ Pour mixture, in several batches, into the container of an electric blender or food processor; process until smooth.

◆ Add cornstarch to yogurt and stir until well-blended. Gradually add yogurt to soup mixture, stirring after each addition. Chill before serving.

(6 SERVINGS)

Add pork and marinade to casserole, stir and loosen pork. Cook 10 minutes.

Pour 4 cups (1 L) chicken broth into casserole and add Tabasco garlic pepper sauce blend, sesame oil, ginger, white pepper, salt, wine and soy sauce.

Raise heat to high, add shrimp and bring to a boil.

◆◆◆◆◆◆◆◆◆◆◆◆◆◆◆◆◆◆◆◆◆◆◆◆◆◆◆

Tainan Noodles

A hot, spicy soup from southern Taiwan.

PORK MARINADE:

1 tsp	**Tabasco garlic pepper sauce blend**	5 mL
3	**Thai chilies, minced**	3
1 tbsp	***each* oyster sauce and mushroom soy sauce**	15 mL
2 tsp	**Shao-Hsing wine or sherry**	10 mL
1 tsp	sesame oil	5 mL
1 tsp	sugar	5 mL

BROTH:

1/2 lb	**fresh ground pork**	225 g
4 1/4 cups	**chicken broth**	1.05 L
1 tbsp	**Tabasco garlic pepper sauce blend**	15 mL
2 tsp	**sesame oil**	10 mL
1	**large piece ginger, 2-in (5-cm) long, crushed**	1
1/4 tsp	**white pepper**	1 mL
	pinch of salt	
2 tsp	**Shao-Hsing wine or sherry**	10 mL
1 tbsp	**soy sauce**	15 mL
12	**large shrimp, washed, shelled and deveined**	12
1/4 lb	**garlic chives or chives cut into 1-inch (2.5-cm) pieces**	115 g
1 lb	**Chinese egg noodles or thin pasta**	450 g

◆ Combine marinade ingredients and add pork and salt to taste. Mix well. Let stand at least 4 hours, stirring occasionally.

◆ Heat a large casserole or wok over high heat, add 1/4 cup (50 mL) of chicken broth and bring to a boil.

◆ Add pork and marinade and cook 10 minutes, stirring constantly, until all liquid is absorbed and meat is very dry and crumbly. Remove cooked pork and set aside.

◆ Pour 4 cups (1 L) chicken broth into casserole and add Tabasco garlic pepper sauce blend, sesame oil, ginger, pepper, salt, wine and soy sauce. Cover and bring to a boil. Lower heat and simmer 4 minutes. Raise heat back to high, add shrimp and bring to a boil.

◆ Meanwhile, bring another pot of water to a boil and add noodles. Boil 1 minute, or until al dente. Rinse and drain noodles twice and divide into 4 large soup bowls.

◆ Add chives to boiling broth and stir briefly until they become bright green; remove from heat. Distribute reserved pork over noodles and ladle broth with shrimp and chives on top. Serve immediately.

(4 SERVINGS)

Cook noodles al dente, rinse and drain twice and divide into 4 large soup bowls.

Distribute reserved pork over noodles.

Ladle broth with shrimp and chives on top of noodles and pork.

Leek and Potato Soup

The touch of jalapeño does wonders for this soup.

¼ cup	butter or margarine	50 mL
2	large leeks, chopped	2
4	all-purpose potatoes, peeled and diced	4
4 cups	chicken broth	1 L
1 tbsp	Tabasco® jalapeño sauce	15 mL
¼ tsp	salt	1 mL
	Sour cream or yogurt	
	Snipped chives	

◆ Melt butter in a 3-qt (3-L) saucepan over medium heat; add leeks. Cook about 5 minutes until tender-crisp. Add potatoes; cook 5 minutes, stirring constantly.

◆ Add chicken broth, Tabasco jalapeño sauce and salt. Bring to a boil over high heat. Reduce heat to low; cover and simmer 15 minutes or until potatoes are tender.

◆ With a food processor or blender, purée soup in batches. To serve, divide into bowls, garnish with a dollop of sour cream or yogurt and top with chives.

(6 SERVINGS)

Turkey and Wild Rice Potage

A delicious way to use cooked turkey.

2 tbsp	butter or margarine	30 mL
2 tbsp	vegetable oil	30 mL
1	large onion, diced	1
1/4 cup	all-purpose flour	50 mL
3 cups	turkey or chicken broth	750 mL
2 cups	diced cooked turkey	500 mL
1 cup	cooked wild or brown rice	250 mL
2 cups	fresh chopped parsley	500 mL
2 tbsp	dry sherry, optional	30 mL
1 tsp	Tabasco® pepper sauce	5 mL
1/4 tsp	salt	1 mL

◆ Heat butter and oil in a 3-quart (3-L) saucepan over medium heat. Add onion and cook until tender, stirring occasionally. With slotted spoon, remove onion to plate.

◆ With a wire whisk, stir flour into drippings remaining in saucepan until well-blended. Cook, stirring constantly, about 5 minutes until mixture is dark brown.

◆ Gradually incorporate turkey broth. Cook over medium-high heat, until mixture thickens slightly and boils. Add turkey, rice, parsley, sherry, Tabasco pepper sauce, salt and cooked onion; simmer 5 minutes to blend flavors, stirring occasionally. Serve.

(4 SERVINGS)

Herb Vegetable Soup

Thyme and mace flavor hearty autumn vegetables.

2 tbsp	margarine or butter	30 mL
1	large onion, chopped	1
1/4 tsp	thyme	1 mL
1/4 tsp	ground mace, divided	1 mL
1 lb	turnips, peeled and cut into 2-inch (5-cm) chunks	450 g
1 lb	new potatoes, peeled and cut into 2-inch (5-cm) chunks	450 g
3 lbs	squash (butternut, Hubbard, pumpkin or acorn), peeled and cubed	1350 g
4 cups	chicken broth	1 L
1/2 tsp	Tabasco® pepper sauce	2 mL

◆ In a 4 to 5-qt (4 to 5-L) saucepan, combine margarine, onions, thyme and half of mace. Cook over medium-high heat, stirring frequently, until onions are translucent, about 5 minutes.

◆ Add turnips, potatoes and squash. Cook over medium heat, stirring occasionally, until vegetables begin to soften, about 30 minutes.

◆ Add broth and Tabasco pepper sauce and bring to a boil over high heat. Reduce heat, cover and simmer until vegetables are very tender, about 30 minutes.

◆ Purée mixture, a portion at a time, with a food processor or blender until smooth. Return to pan and heat until steaming hot. Sprinkle individual servings with remaining mace.

(8 SERVINGS)

◆ ◆ ◆ ◆ ◆ ◆ ◆ ◆ ◆ ◆ ◆ ◆ ◆ ◆ ◆ ◆ ◆ ◆ ◆ ◆

Seafood Gumbo

This is a roux-based New Orleans version of Louisiana's famous dish.

5 tbsp	vegetable oil	75 mL
1 lb	fresh okra, thinly sliced	450 g
1 tsp	white vinegar	5 mL
1/3 cup	all-purpose flour	75 mL
1 cup	chopped onion	250 mL
1 cup	chopped green onions	250 mL
2	cloves garlic, minced	2
1 cup	chopped green pepper	250 mL
1/2 cup	chopped celery	125 mL
2 tbsp	chopped fresh parsley	30 mL
2 cups	canned whole tomatoes, undrained and chopped	500 mL
1/2 cup	cubed cooked ham	125 mL
1 1/2 qts	fish stock or water	1.5 L
2	bay leaves	2
1	fresh thyme sprig	1
1 tbsp	Worcestershire sauce	15 mL
1 tsp	Tabasco® pepper sauce	5 mL
1 tsp	salt	5 mL
1 lb	shrimp, shelled and deveined	450 g
1/2 lb	crab meat	225 g
3 cups	cooked rice	750 mL
	Chopped green onions and fresh parsley	

◆ Heat 3 tbsp (45 mL) of oil in a medium skillet (not cast iron).

◆ Add okra and cook 30 minutes, stirring frequently, over medium heat. Add vinegar and cook another 10 minutes, until okra is no longer sticky and is lightly browned. Set aside.

◆ Heat remaining 2 tbsp (30 mL) of oil in a large pot. Add flour and cook over medium heat, stirring constantly, about 30 minutes, until roux turns dark brown and develops a nutty aroma.

◆ Add onion, green onions, garlic, green pepper, celery and parsley, and cook 10 minutes, or until vegetables are tender.

◆ Add tomatoes, okra, ham, fish stock, bay leaves, thyme, Worcestershire sauce, Tabasco pepper sauce and salt. Simmer, uncovered, 45 minutes.

◆ Add shrimp and crab meat and simmer 5 to 10 minutes. Discard bay leaves and thyme. Serve gumbo over cooked rice with additional Tabasco pepper sauce, if desired. Garnish with green onions and parsley.

(6 SERVINGS)

♦ Salads ♦

◆◆◆◆◆◆◆◆◆◆◆◆◆◆◆◆◆◆◆◆◆◆◆◆

Mango Salad

A wonderfully refreshing combination.

4	large ripe mangoes, peeled and diced	4
1 cup	jicama*, peeled and diced	250 mL
1/2 cup	chopped red pepper	125 mL
2 tbsp	chopped cilantro	30 mL
1 tbsp	fresh lime juice	15 mL
	Lettuce leaves	
6	thin slices of red onion, separated into rings	6
	Creamy Orange Jalapeño Dressing	

◆ In a medium bowl, combine mango, jicama, red pepper, cilantro and lime juice. Toss gently but thoroughly. Cover and chill.

◆ Arrange lettuce leaves on 6 salad plates. Mound 1/2 cup mango mixture in center of each plate. Drizzle 1 1/2 tbsp (25 mL) of Creamy Orange Jalapeño Dressing over each salad. Garnish with red onion rings.

* *Also known as the Mexican potato, jicama is a large, bulbous root vegetable with a sweet nutty flavor. It is available in many large supermarkets, but if you cannot find it, you can use water chestnuts to provide a similar crunchy texture to this salad.*

(6 SERVINGS)

Creamy Orange Jalapeño Dressing

1/3 cup	"crema Mexicana" Mexican-style whipping cream*	75 mL
3 tbsp	frozen orange juice concentrate	45 mL
3 tbsp	milk	45 mL
1 tbsp	Tabasco® jalapeño sauce	15 mL

◆ In a small bowl, whisk all ingredients until well blended. Cover and refrigerate until ready to serve.

* *A mixture of half sour cream and half whipping cream may be substituted for crema Mexicana in this recipe.*

(2/3 CUP – 150 ML)

◆◆◆◆◆◆◆◆◆◆◆◆◆◆◆◆◆◆◆◆◆◆◆

Potato Salad with Sweet Sausages and Mushrooms

A hearty salad for cold weather appetites.

3 lbs	small red potatoes, quartered	1.4 kg
2 lbs	sweet Italian sausages	900 g
1/2 cup	dry red wine	125 mL
2/3 cup, 2 tbsp	extra-virgin olive oil	180 mL
1 lb	mushrooms, sliced	450 g
1 tsp	fresh lemon juice	5 mL
1 tbsp	Tabasco® pepper sauce, divided	15 mL
3/4 cup	chopped green onions	175 mL
2 tbsp	Dijon mustard	30 mL
1/2 tsp	salt	2 mL
1/4 tsp	black pepper	1 mL
1/3 cup	dry white wine	75 mL
1/3 cup	chicken stock or broth	75 mL

◆ Boil potatoes in a large saucepan over medium-high heat, 15 to 20 minutes, or until tender. Drain and allow to cool to room temperature before slicing into 1/4-inch (5-mm) slices. Place potatoes in a large bowl.

◆ Meanwhile, preheat oven to 350°F (180°C). Line a baking dish with sausages and prick them several times with a fork. Bake 15 minutes; turn and bake 15 minutes.

◆ Add red wine to dish, turn sausages and bake 8 minutes. Turn sausages once more and bake 7 minutes or until cooked through. Remove sausages and let cool. Slice into 1-inch (2.5 cm) rings and add to potatoes.

◆ Heat 2 tbsp (30 mL) of olive oil in a large skillet. Add mushrooms and sauté over moderately high heat, tossing until liquid evaporates, about 5 minutes. Sprinkle in lemon juice and half of Tabasco pepper sauce. Add to potato mixture. Stir in green onions.

◆ In a food processor or blender, combine mustard, salt, pepper, remaining Tabasco pepper sauce, white wine and stock. Blend to mix well. With machine on, slowly add remaining 2/3 cup (150 mL) olive oil.

◆ Pour dressing over salad and toss to coat. Serve warm or at room temperature, or cover and refrigerate overnight.

(12 SERVINGS)

Cracked Wheat Salad

A delicious version of Middle-Eastern tabbouleh.

1/2 cup	cracked wheat	125 mL
1 1/2 cups	water	375 mL
2 cups	chopped parsley	500 mL
1/2 cup	chopped mint	125 mL
1/2 cup	thinly sliced whole green onions	125 mL
2 cups	peeled, diced tomatoes	500 mL
1/4 cup	olive oil	50 mL
1/4 cup	lemon juice	50 mL
1/2 tsp	salt	2 mL
1/2 tsp	Tabasco® pepper sauce	2 mL

◆ Soak wheat in water until tender, about 30 minutes.

◆ In a large bowl, toss together parsley, mint, green onions and tomatoes. Drain wheat well and add to ingredients in bowl.

◆ Beat together remaining ingredients and pour over wheat and vegetables; mix well. Serve on large lettuce leaves.

(6 SERVINGS)

Seafood Orzo Salad

A light, elegant dish for summer dining.

1 cup	orzo (rice-shaped pasta)	250 mL
2 tbsp	olive oil	30 mL
1/2 lb	medium shrimp, peeled and deveined	225 g
1/2 lb	bay scallops	225 g
1	clove garlic, minced	1
2	green onions, sliced	2
2 tbsp	fresh chopped dill	30 mL
1 tbsp	lemon juice	15 mL
1 tsp	salt	5 mL
1 tsp	Tabasco® pepper sauce	5 mL

◆ Prepare orzo according to package directions. Drain.

◆ Meanwhile, heat 1 tbsp (15 mL) of olive oil in a 12-inch (30-cm) skillet over medium-high heat. Add shrimp, scallops and garlic and cook 5 minutes or until seafood is tender, stirring occasionally.

◆ In a large bowl, toss seafood mixture, orzo, green onions, dill, lemon juice, salt, Tabasco pepper sauce and 1 tbsp (15 mL) oil until well-mixed. Serve immediately or refrigerate to serve cold.

(4 SERVINGS)

◆ ◆

Mexican Chicken Salad

The spicy flavor goes well with cool avocado.

2 cups	cooked chicken, cubed	500 mL
1/4 cup	sour cream	50 mL
1/4 cup	mayonnaise	50 mL
1/4 cup	finely chopped carrot	50 mL
2 tbsp	cilantro	30 mL
2 tbsp	capers, drained	30 mL
2 tbsp	finely chopped red bell pepper	30 mL
2 tbsp	lemon juice	30 mL
1/4 tsp	ground cumin	1 mL
1/4 cup	finely chopped onion	50 mL
4 tbsp	Tabasco® jalapeño sauce	60 mL
	Salt to taste	
1	avocado, peeled and cut into wedges	1
	Lettuce leaves	
	Paprika	

◆ Toss together all ingredients except avocado, lettuce and paprika.

◆ Serve on lettuce leaves with avocado wedges. Sprinkle with paprika. Add more jalapeño sauce, if desired, and serve.

(4 SERVINGS)

Tuscan Summer Salad

The Italians call this panzanella. The stale bread soaks up the dressing and tomato juices.

1	small loaf coarse Italian bread, stale	1
1/4 cup	olive oil	50 mL
3 tbsp	balsamic vinegar	45 mL
1	clove garlic, crushed	1
1 tsp	salt	5 mL
1 tsp	Tabasco® pepper sauce	5 mL
3	large ripe tomatoes, cut into large chunks	3
1	large red onion, cut in half and sliced	1
1	large cucumber, cut into large chunks	1
1	large red pepper, seeded and cut into large pieces	1
1	large yellow pepper, seeded and cut into large pieces	1
1 cup	arugula leaves	250 mL
1/2 cup	fresh basil leaves	125 mL
1/2 cup	black olives	125 mL
1 tbsp	capers	15 mL

◆ Tear bread into large pieces to make about 4 cups (1 L).

◆ In a large bowl, combine olive oil, balsamic vinegar, garlic, salt and Tabasco pepper sauce.

◆ Add remaining ingredients, including bread; toss to mix well. Let salad stand 30 minutes and serve.

(4 SERVINGS)

◆◆◆◆◆◆◆◆◆◆◆◆◆◆◆◆◆◆◆◆◆◆◆◆

Shrimp and Rice with Spicy Vinaigrette

A main dish salad flavored with feta.

2 tbsp	vegetable oil, divided	30 mL
1 lb	large shrimp, peeled and deveined	450 g
1	large clove garlic, minced	1
2	green onions, sliced	2
2 cups	water	500 mL
1 cup	long-grain rice	250 mL
1 tsp	salt	5 mL
1	medium cucumber, diced	1
½ cup	crumbled feta cheese	125 mL

SPICY VINAIGRETTE:

¼ cup	olive oil	50 mL
3 tbsp	cider vinegar	45 mL
1 tbsp	Dijon mustard	15 mL
1 tsp	Tabasco® pepper sauce	5 mL
1 tsp	salt	5 mL

◆ Heat 1 tbsp (15 mL) of oil in a 3-qt (3-L) saucepan over medium-high heat. Cook half the shrimp, until well-browned and tender. With slotted spoon, remove to a large bowl. Repeat with remaining shrimp and oil.

◆ Reduce heat to medium. In liquid remaining in saucepan, cook garlic and green onions about 2 minutes, stirring frequently.

◆ Add water, rice and salt to saucepan. Bring to a boil over high heat. Reduce heat to low; cover and simmer 20 minutes or until rice is tender. Meanwhile, add cucumber and feta cheese to bowl containing shrimp.

◆ Prepare vinaigrette by combining all ingredients in a small bowl. Add rice and vinaigrette to shrimp mixture and toss to mix well. Serve.

(6 SERVINGS)

◆◆◆◆◆◆◆◆◆◆◆◆◆◆◆◆◆◆◆◆◆◆◆◆

Cajun Potato Salad

The egg yolks are in the dressing.

2¹/₂ lbs	medium red potatoes, peeled and cut into quarters	1125 g
1 tsp	salt	5 mL
6	hard-boiled eggs	6
¹/₄ cup	oil	50 mL
¹/₂ tsp	white vinegar	2 mL
1 cup	mayonnaise	250 mL
¹/₈ tsp	cayenne pepper	0.5 mL
1 tsp	Tabasco® pepper sauce	5 mL
1	sweet pickle, chopped fine	1
¹/₂	stalk celery, chopped	¹/₂
¹/₄	green bell pepper, chopped	¹/₄

◆ Fill a 2-qt (2-L) saucepan ²/₃ full of cold water. Add potatoes and salt. Cook over medium heat until potatoes are tender; drain.

◆ Peel eggs; separate whites and yolks. In a large bowl, mash yolks with oil and vinegar. Add mayonnaise, cayenne pepper and Tabasco pepper sauce.

◆ Dice potatoes and add to yolk mixture along with pickle, celery and bell pepper. Cut egg whites into small pieces and add to salad. Stir to mix. Refrigerate until ready to serve.

(8 SERVINGS)

Corn Seafood Salad

Some of America's favorite foods in one great salad.

2 cups	cooked corn	500 mL
1	green pepper, diced	1
1	medium tomato, diced	1
1 lb	shrimp, cooked and cleaned or 1¹/₂ cups (375 mL) crab meat	450 g
¹/₃ cup	mayonnaise	75 mL
1 tbsp	minced onion	15 mL
¹/₂ tsp	Tabasco® pepper sauce	2 mL
1 tsp	salt	5 mL

◆ Combine corn, green pepper, tomato and shrimp.

◆ Blend mayonnaise, onion, Tabasco pepper sauce and salt. Add to corn mixture and toss gently.

◆ Chill before serving. Garnish with tomato wedges.

(4 SERVINGS)

◆ ◆

Cool Fruit and Vegetable Salad with Hot Tomato Dip

A delightful and unusual combination.

2	**medium tomatoes**	2
¼ cup	**olive oil**	**50 mL**
2 tbsp	**red wine vinegar**	**30 mL**
1 tsp	**Tabasco® pepper sauce**	**5 mL**
3	**cilantro sprigs**	3
¼ tsp	**salt**	**1 mL**
1	**small head green leaf lettuce**	1
4	**large slices honeydew melon**	4
1	**large navel orange, peeled and sliced**	1
1	**medium cucumber, thinly sliced**	1
1	**red bell pepper, cut into thin strips**	1
6	**small green onions**	6

◆ With a food processor or blender, combine tomatoes, oil, vinegar, Tabasco pepper sauce, cilantro and salt. Process until smooth. Refrigerate until ready to serve.

◆ Arrange lettuce leaves on a large platter. Top with melon, orange and cucumber slices, red pepper strips and green onions. Serve with dip.

(6 SERVINGS)

Chicken and Brown Rice Salad

Brown rice and pecans lend nutty flavor and texture to this excellent main dish salad.

2 tbsp	butter	30 mL
2	cloves garlic, chopped	2
1	small onion, chopped	1
1 cup	brown rice	250 mL
2 cups	chicken broth	500 mL
2 cups	cooked, diced chicken	500 mL
1 cup	shredded carrots	250 mL
1/2 cup	raisins	125 mL
1/3 cup	chopped green onions	75 mL
1/3 cup	olive oil	75 mL
1/4 cup	white wine vinegar	50 mL
2 tsp	Dijon mustard	10 mL
1	clove garlic, minced	1
1/2 tsp	Tabasco® pepper sauce	2 mL
1/2 cup	toasted pecans	125 mL

◆ In a medium saucepan, melt butter and sauté chopped garlic and onion until golden, about 2 minutes. Add rice and sauté, stirring constantly, until rice is browned. Add broth and mix well. Cover and simmer 35 minutes or until broth is absorbed and rice is tender.

◆ Transfer rice to a large bowl and let cool. Mix in chicken, carrots, raisins and green onions.

◆ In a small bowl, whisk together oil, vinegar, mustard, minced garlic and Tabasco pepper sauce. Pour over rice salad, mix well and refrigerate 2 to 3 hours to blend flavors. Stir in pecans and serve.

(4-6 SERVINGS)

◆ ◆

Seasonal Greens with Warm Ham and Shrimp in Spicy Orange Dressing

A delightful main dish for warm weather.

DRESSING:

1¹/₂	medium oranges, peeled and sectioned	1¹/₂
5 tbsp	vegetable oil	75 mL
2 tbsp	wine vinegar	30 mL
2 tsp	chopped fresh basil	10 mL
2 tsp	chopped fresh parsley	10 mL
1¹/₂ tsp	Tabasco® pepper sauce	7 mL
1	small clove garlic	1
	Salt and freshly ground pepper to taste	

SALAD:

18	large shrimp, peeled and deveined	18
4 oz	country ham, cut into thin strips	120 g
1	large carrot, pared and cut into thin strips	1
1	medium sweet red pepper, seeded and cut into thin strips	1
1	medium sweet yellow pepper, seeded and cut into thin strips	1
1	small red onion, halved and thinly sliced	1
1	medium head red leaf lettuce, leaves separated and kept whole	1
1	medium head chicory lettuce*, cut into bite-size pieces	1
1 lb	mixed lettuce (spinach, watercress, Belgian endive and/or arugula), leaves only	450 g
2 tbsp	olive oil	30 mL

◆ With a blender or food processor, combine oranges, vegetable oil, vinegar, basil, parsley, Tabasco pepper sauce and garlic. Process until mixture is thoroughly blended, about 1 minute. Transfer dressing to a bowl and season with salt and pepper.

◆ Combine shrimp, ham, carrot, red and yellow peppers and onion; set aside. Just before serving, arrange red leaf lettuce on 6 large plates. Place chicory and mixed lettuce on top.

◆ Heat a 12-inch (30-cm) skillet over high heat. Add olive oil and heat until lightly smoking. Add shrimp and vegetable mixture. Stir-fry until shrimp is cooked through, 3 to 3¹/₂ minutes. Add dressing. Toss mixture to combine all ingredients and heat dressing, 20 to 30 seconds.

◆ Spoon shrimp mixture and dressing evenly over the prepared greens. Serve immediately.

* *All lettuce should be trimmed, well-rinsed and dried.*

(6 SERVINGS)

◆ Pasta and Rice ◆

Capellini with Sweet and Spicy Shrimp

Cherries and brandy make this an interesting dish.

1 lb	capellini or angel hair pasta	450 g
1/2 lb	butter	225 g
1 cup	diced onion	250 mL
8	cloves garlic, minced	8
2 lbs	medium shrimp, peeled and deveined	900 g
1 cup	chicken broth	250 mL
4 oz	sun-dried cherries	115 g
1/3 cup	lemon juice	75 mL
3 oz	cherry brandy or brandy	90 g
2 tbsp	Tabasco® pepper sauce	30 mL
1 tsp	salt	5 mL
1 cup	fresh basil, cut in thin strips	250 mL
4 oz	grated fresh Parmesan or Asiago cheese	115 g
	Fresh basil sprigs and whole cherries for garnish, optional	

◆ In a large pot of boiling water, prepare pasta according to package directions. Drain well.

◆ Meanwhile, melt butter in a large skillet, over medium heat. Cook onion and garlic 5 minutes or until translucent, stirring occasionally.

◆ Add shrimp and sauté 3 minutes, until shrimp are done. Remove and set aside.

◆ Add chicken broth, sun-dried cherries, lemon juice, brandy, Tabasco pepper sauce and salt. Bring to a boil over high heat. Reduce heat to low and simmer 2 minutes to blend flavors.

◆ Stir in 1/2 cup (125 mL) fresh basil, 2 oz (60 g) Parmesan cheese, and reserved shrimp.

◆ Place pasta on platter; top with shrimp mixture. Sprinkle with remaining basil strips and Parmesan. Serve garnished with basil sprigs and whole cherries, if desired.

(6 SERVINGS)

◆◆◆◆◆◆◆◆◆◆◆◆◆◆◆◆◆◆◆◆◆◆◆◆

Risotto with Vegetables

Diners should wait for this dish – not the other way around.

1½ tbsp	margarine	25 mL
1½ tbsp	olive oil	25 mL
1 cup	sliced mushrooms	250 mL
½ cup	chopped onion	125 mL
1	clove garlic, minced	1
1 cup	uncooked Arborio rice	250 mL
	Pinch saffron (optional)	
2 cups	hot low-sodium chicken broth	500 mL
½ tsp	Tabasco® pepper sauce	2 mL
1½ cups	hot water, divided	375 mL
1	9-oz (270-g) package frozen artichoke hearts, cooked and drained	1
½ cup	coarsely chopped roasted red peppers*	125 mL

◆ Heat margarine and oil in a large skillet over medium heat. Add mushrooms, onion and garlic; cook 5 minutes or until onions are translucent.

◆ Stir in rice; cook 1 to 2 minutes or until partly translucent. Add saffron, if desired. Add ½ cup (125 mL) of hot broth and Tabasco pepper sauce; stir constantly until rice absorbs broth.

◆ Add remaining broth and hot water, ½ cup (125 mL) at a time, stirring constantly from bottom and sides of pan. (Wait until rice begins to dry out before adding more liquid.)

◆ Cook and stir about 30 minutes, or until rice is tender but firm and the risotto is the consistency of creamy rice pudding. (The total amount of liquid used will vary. Watch rice carefully to ensure proper consistency.)

◆ Stir in artichokes and roasted peppers. Serve with additional Tabasco pepper sauce, if desired.

* *To prepare peppers, prick with fork and roast until skin blisters. Cool slightly; peel and chop.*

(6 SERVINGS)

Sesame Noodles

Delicious warm or cold.

1 lb	spaghetti	450 g
1 cup	chunky peanut butter	250 mL
1 cup	orange juice	250 mL
1/4 cup	soy sauce	50 mL
1/4 cup	sesame oil	50 mL
1/4 cup	vegetable oil	50 mL
2 tbsp	cider vinegar	30 mL
1 tbsp	Tabasco® pepper sauce	15 mL
1 tsp	salt	5 mL
2	large green onions, sliced	2
1	medium cucumber, sliced	1

◆ Prepare spaghetti according to package directions. Drain.

◆ Meanwhile, in a large bowl, whisk together peanut butter, orange juice, soy sauce, sesame oil, vegetable oil, cider vinegar, Tabasco pepper sauce and salt until smooth. Add cooked spaghetti and green onions; toss well.

◆ Serve warm or cover and refrigerate to serve cold. Just before serving, toss with additional orange juice, if necessary, and garnish with cucumber slices.

(6 SERVINGS)

Pasta with Roasted Vegetables

Wonderful texture and taste.

1	**2-lb (900-g) butternut squash, peeled, seeded, and cut into 1-inch (2.5-cm) cubes**	1
10 oz	**fresh Brussels sprouts, each cut in half**	300 g
1	**small bulb fennel, trimmed, halved and thinly sliced**	1
3	**large cloves garlic, peeled and halved lengthwise**	3
1/4 cup	**olive oil**	50 mL
3/4 tsp	**salt**	3 mL
1/2 tsp	**dried oregano**	2 mL
1/4 cup	**pumpkin seeds**	50 mL
8 oz	**penne or ziti pasta**	240 g
1 tbsp	**Tabasco® garlic pepper sauce blend**	15 mL
1/2 cup	**grated Parmesan cheese**	125 mL

◆ Preheat oven to 450°F (230°C). In a roasting pan, combine squash, Brussels sprouts, fennel, garlic, olive oil, salt and oregano. Bake 20 minutes, stirring occasionally. During last 2 minutes of roasting, add pumpkin seeds; cook until lightly toasted.

◆ Meanwhile, prepare penne or ziti according to package directions.

◆ When done, drain pasta and toss with roasted vegetables, Tabasco garlic pepper sauce blend and Parmesan cheese to mix well. Serve immediately.

(4 SERVINGS)

◆◆◆◆◆◆◆◆◆◆◆◆◆◆◆◆◆◆◆◆◆◆◆

Barley-Vegetable Pilaf

Delicious served with lamb or beef.

2 tbsp	margarine	30 mL
1	medium onion, diced	1
4 oz	mushrooms, sliced	120 g
1 cup	reduced sodium chicken or beef broth	250 mL
1/2 cup	pearl barley	125 mL
1 tsp	Tabasco® pepper sauce	5 mL
1	medium red bell pepper, diced	1
1	medium zucchini, sliced	1

◆ Melt margarine in a 10-inch (25-cm) skillet over medium heat. Add onion and mushrooms and cook 5 minutes, stirring occasionally.

◆ Add broth, barley and Tabasco pepper sauce. Bring to a boil over high heat. Reduce heat to low; cover and simmer 20 minutes.

◆ Add red pepper and zucchini; cover and simmer 15 to 20 minutes or until barley is tender, stirring occasionally. Serve hot or cold.

(3-4 SERVINGS)

Jalapeño Green Rice

This packs a real flavor punch.

1	chile poblano, peeled and seeded*	1
1/2	medium onion	1/2
1/2 cup	loosely packed parsley	125 mL
2	cloves garlic	2
2 cups	chicken stock, divided	500 mL
1 tbsp	vegetable oil	15 mL
1 cup	uncooked rice	250 mL
1 tbsp	Tabasco® jalapeño sauce	15 mL
1/2 tsp	salt	2 mL

◆ With a blender, combine chile poblano, onion, parsley and garlic with 1/2 cup (125 mL) chicken stock; blend until smooth. Set aside.

◆ Heat oil in a 3-qt (3-L) skillet over medium-high heat. Add rice and cook until golden, stirring constantly.

◆ Add remaining chicken stock, puréed mixture, Tabasco jalapeño sauce and salt. Bring to a boil; stir once or twice. Reduce heat, cover and simmer 20 minutes, or until rice is tender and liquid is absorbed.

* *Roast chile over a gas burner, under a broiler or on a griddle, turning until skin is blistered and charred on all sides. Place in a plastic bag; close and let steam 15 minutes. Remove skin under running water. Slit pepper to open; wash out seeds and remove veins.*

(6 SERVINGS)

◆◆◆◆◆◆◆◆◆◆◆◆◆◆◆◆◆◆◆◆

Paella

This dish can also be simmered on the stove in a heavy skillet with a tight fitting lid.

1	3-lb (1.4-kg) chicken, cut in pieces	1
1¼ tsp	salt, divided	6 mL
½ tsp	paprika	2 mL
4 tbsp	olive oil	60 mL
½ lb	ham, diced	225 g
1	medium onion, chopped	1
½ cup	diced green pepper	125 mL
2 cups	canned peas with liquid	500 mL
1½ cups	beer	375 mL
½ tsp	Tabasco® pepper sauce	2 mL
2	chicken bouillon cubes	2
¼ tsp	saffron	1 mL
1½ cups	uncooked rice	375 mL
6	mussels	6
6	clams	6
½ lb	shrimp, cooked and shelled	225 g
2	pimiento peppers, cut in pieces	2

◆ Preheat oven to 350°F (180°C).

◆ Sprinkle chicken with 1 tsp (5 mL) of salt and paprika. Heat olive oil in skillet and brown chicken; remove to baking dish with tight-fitting lid.

◆ Cook ham in skillet and add to chicken. Cook onion and green pepper until onion is tender, but not brown.

◆ Drain liquid from peas into a large measuring cup; add beer and enough water to make 3 cups (750 mL). Add Tabasco pepper sauce. Stir liquid into skillet, scraping brown particles from bottom of pan. Add bouillon cubes, saffron and remaining ¼ tsp (1 mL) salt. Bring to a boil and pour over chicken and ham.

◆ Sprinkle rice over chicken and stir until all rice is moistened. Cover tightly and bake 25 minutes.

◆ Uncover and toss rice. Arrange mussels, clams, shrimp, pimientos and peas on top of rice. Cover and return to oven. Bake 10 minutes and serve.

(6 SERVINGS)

Heat olive oil in skillet and brown chicken; remove to baking dish with tight-fitting lid.

Cook ham in skillet and add to chicken.

Cook onion and green pepper until onion is tender, but not brown.

Add Tabasco pepper sauce to liquid and stir into skillet, scraping brown particles from bottom of pan.

Bring bouillon mixture to a boil and pour over chicken and ham.

Sprinkle rice over chicken and stir until all rice is moistened.

◆◆◆◆◆◆◆◆◆◆◆◆◆◆◆◆◆◆◆◆◆◆◆◆

Linguine with Spinach Pesto Sauce

Try this when fresh basil isn't available.

4 cups	loosely packed fresh spinach leaves	1 L
3/4 cup	grated Parmesan cheese	175 mL
1/2 cup	walnuts	125 mL
1/4 cup	olive oil	50 mL
l	large clove garlic	1
2 tsp	dried basil leaves	10 mL
1 tbsp	Tabasco® garlic pepper sauce blend	15 mL
1/2 tsp	salt	2 mL
16 oz	linguine, cooked	480 g

◆ With a food processor or blender, combine spinach, 1/2 cup (125 ml) Parmesan cheese, walnuts, olive oil, garlic, basil, Tabasco garlic pepper sauce blend and salt. Process until mixture is smooth. Makes 1 cup (250 mL) spinach pesto.

◆ Toss pesto with cooked linguine to mix well. Serve with remaining 1/4 cup (50 mL) cheese.

(6 SERVINGS)

Spaghetti Puttanesca

Intense flavor for pasta lovers.

5 tbsp	olive oil	75 mL
2	cloves garlic, minced	2
4	anchovy fillets, coarsely chopped	4
1	28-oz (796-g) can whole plum tomatoes, drained and chopped	1
2 tbsp	tomato paste	30 mL
2 tbsp	capers, rinsed and drained	30 mL
3/4 tsp	Tabasco® pepper sauce	3 mL
3/4 tsp	dried oregano, crumbled	3 mL
1/2 cup	Italian or Greek cured black olives, pitted and sliced	125 mL
2 tbsp	chopped fresh parsley	30 mL
12 oz	spaghetti, cooked and drained	360 g

◆ Heat oil in a medium skillet. Sauté garlic and anchovy fillets 3 minutes, stirring frequently.

◆ Stir in tomatoes, tomato paste, capers, Tabasco pepper sauce and oregano; simmer 5 minutes, stirring occasionally. Stir in olives and parsley; simmer 2 minutes.

◆ Toss with hot spaghetti in a large bowl. Serve with additional Tabasco pepper sauce, if desired.

(4 SERVINGS)

◆◆◆◆◆◆◆◆◆◆◆◆◆◆◆◆◆◆◆◆◆◆◆

Chicken Lasagna Primavera

1 lb	boneless, skinless chicken breasts or thighs	450 g
3 tbsp	olive oil	45 mL
1 tsp	salt	5 mL
1	large onion, diced	1
3/4 lb	mushrooms, sliced	350 g
1/2 cup	butter or margarine	125 mL
4 cups	shredded zucchini	1 L
3 cups	shredded carrot	750 mL
1/2 cup	all-purpose flour	125 mL
13/4 cups	chicken broth	425 mL
1/2 cup	milk	125 mL
2 tsp	Tabasco® pepper sauce	10 mL
1/8 tsp	ground nutmeg	0.5 mL
2 cups	ricotta cheese	500 mL
8 oz	feta cheese, crumbled	225 g
9	pre-cooked lasagna noodles	9
2 cups	shredded Monterey Jack cheese	500 mL

◆ Cut chicken into thin strips. Heat 1 tbsp (15 mL) of oil in a large skillet over medium-high heat. Add chicken with half of salt; cook until browned and tender, stirring frequently. Remove to bowl.

◆ Over medium heat, heat remaining oil in same skillet and sauté onion and mushrooms. Add to chicken.

◆ Heat 2 tbsp (30 mL) butter in same skillet over medium heat; add zucchini. Cook 3 to 5 minutes until tender and liquid has evaporated, stirring frequently. Remove to bowl. Repeat procedure with carrots and remove to another bowl.

◆ Melt remaining butter. Stir in flour and cook 2 minutes. Gradually incorporate chicken broth and milk, stirring until mixture thickens. Add Tabasco pepper sauce, nutmeg and remaining salt.

◆ Preheat oven to 350°F (180°C). In a medium bowl, stir together ricotta and feta cheese.

◆ In a large baking dish, spread 1/4 of sauce; top with 3 dry noodles, being careful not to touch outsides of dish. Cover noodles completely with 1/4 of sauce. Top with 1/2 of zucchini, 1/2 of carrots, 1/2 of feta-cheese mixture, 1/2 of chicken mixture and 1/3 Monterey Jack cheese. Repeat to make a second layer.

◆ Make final layer with remaining noodles, sauce, and Jack cheese. Cover dish with foil and bake 30 minutes. Remove foil and bake 10 minutes, or until mixture is hot and bubbly. Let cool slightly.

(8 SERVINGS)

Cover noodles completely with 1/4 of sauce.

Top with 1/2 of zucchini.

Cover with 1/2 of carrots.

Top with $1/2$ of feta-cheese mixture.

Spoon $1/2$ of chicken mixture on top.

Finish each layer with $1/3$ Monterey Jack cheese.

◆◆◆◆◆◆◆◆◆◆◆◆◆◆◆◆◆◆◆◆◆◆◆

Hopping John

Serve on New Year's Day for good luck.

1 lb	dried black-eyed peas	450 g
1/2 lb	sliced salt pork or bacon	225 g
1 tsp	Tabasco® pepper sauce	5 mL
1/2 tsp	salt	2 mL
2 tbsp	bacon drippings	30 mL
2	medium onions, chopped	2
1 cup	uncooked long-grain rice	250 mL
1 1/2 cups	boiling water	375 mL

◆ In a large kettle, cover peas with 6 cups (1.5 L) cold water. Soak overnight*.

◆ Add salt pork, Tabasco pepper sauce and salt. Cover and cook over low heat about 30 minutes.

◆ Meanwhile, cook onions in bacon drippings until transparent, about 5 minutes. Add to peas with rice and boiling water. Cook until rice is tender and water is absorbed, about 20 minutes, stirring occasionally. Serve hot.

* Another method to rehydrate peas, is to bring them to a boil, simmer 2 minutes and let them stand 1 hour.

(8 SERVINGS)

Savory Sausage and Spinach Penne

A hearty single-dish meal.

20 oz	penne	600 g
2 tbsp	olive oil	30 mL
3	cloves garlic, minced	3
1 lb	sweet sausage meat, casing removed	450 g
1 lb	fresh spinach	450 g
1 cup	crushed tomatoes	250 mL
¹/₂ cup	chicken broth	125 mL
¹/₂ cup	dry white wine	125 mL
³/₄ cup	oil packed sun-dried tomatoes, chopped or ¹/₄ cup (50 mL) dry sun-dried tomatoes, chopped	175 mL
1 tbsp	fresh chopped basil or 1 tsp (5 mL) dried basil	15 mL
2 tsp	Tabasco® pepper sauce	10 mL
	Salt and pepper to taste	
	Parmesan cheese to taste	

◆ Cook pasta according to package directions and set aside.

◆ Heat oil in a large skillet over medium-high heat, sauté garlic until lightly browned. Add crumbled sausage, sauté 4 minutes then push to the sides of the pan.

◆ Add spinach, sauté until tender, about 3 minutes. Add crushed tomatoes, chicken broth, wine, sun-dried tomatoes, basil and Tabasco pepper sauce; let cook 5 minutes.

◆ Remove sausage mixture from heat and toss lightly with cooked pasta. Season with salt and pepper. Sprinkle with Parmesan cheese and serve.

(4 SERVINGS)

◆◆◆◆◆◆◆◆◆◆◆◆◆◆◆◆◆◆◆◆◆◆◆◆

Risotto Milanese

This creamy rice dish is a real treat.

1	**small onion, thinly sliced**	1
1 tbsp	**margarine**	15 mL
1 cup	**uncooked Arborio rice**	250 mL
	Pinch saffron	
½ cup	**dry white wine**	125 mL
¼ tsp	**Tabasco® pepper sauce**	1 mL
2 cups	**low-sodium chicken broth**	500 mL
¼ cup	**grated Parmesan cheese**	50 mL
	Salt and freshly ground white pepper to taste	

◆ In a large skillet, sauté onion in margarine over medium-high heat. Add rice and saffron; stir constantly 2 to 3 minutes.

◆ Add wine and Tabasco pepper sauce; stir until absorbed. Stir in one cup (250 mL) of broth. Cook, uncovered, stirring frequently until broth is absorbed.

◆ Add remaining broth, ½ cup (125 mL) at a time, stirring constantly from bottom and sides of pan. (Wait until rice begins to dry out before adding more liquid.)

◆ Cook and stir until rice is tender but firm and the risotto is the consistency of creamy rice pudding. (The total amount of liquid used will vary. Watch rice carefully to ensure proper consistency.)

◆ Stir in cheese, salt and pepper, and serve immediately.

(6 SERVINGS)

Add rice and saffron; stir constantly 2 to 3 minutes.

Add wine and Tabasco pepper sauce; stir until absorbed.

Stir in one cup (250 mL) of broth. Cook, uncovered, stirring frequently until broth is absorbed.

◆◆◆◆◆◆◆◆◆◆◆◆◆◆◆◆◆◆◆◆◆◆◆◆◆

Baked Macaroni, Sausage and Cheese

A comfortable casserole dish.

3 cups	elbow macaroni	750 mL
1 lb	hot or sweet Italian sausage	450 g
1	large green pepper, diced	1
1	large onion, diced	1
3 tbsp	butter or margarine	45 mL
3 tbsp	all-purpose flour	45 mL
2 cups	milk	500 mL
2 cups	shredded sharp cheddar cheese	500 mL
1/4 cup	grated Parmesan cheese	50 mL
1 1/4 tsp	Tabasco® pepper sauce	6 mL
1 tsp	salt	5 mL

◆ Cook elbow macaroni according to package directions. Drain and rinse with cold water; drain again.

◆ Meanwhile, in a 12-inch (30-cm) skillet over medium-high heat, cook sausages, turning frequently, until well-browned on all sides and cooked through, about 15 minutes. Remove sausages to cutting board.

◆ Add green pepper and onion to drippings remaining in skillet. Cook over medium heat until tender, about 8 minutes, stirring occasionally. With slotted spoon, remove to a large bowl.

◆ When sausages are cool enough to handle, cut into 1/2-inch (1-cm) slices; remove to bowl with vegetables.

◆ Preheat oven to 375°F (190°C). Melt butter in a 2-qt (2-L) saucepan over medium heat. Stir in flour; cook 1 minute. Gradually whisk in milk. Bring to a boil, stirring frequently. Remove from heat. Add remaining ingredients and stir constantly until cheeses melt.

◆ Combine cheddar cheese sauce, macaroni and sausage mixture. Spoon into greased 12 × 8-inch (30 × 20-cm) baking dish. Bake 20 to 25 minutes, or until mixture is hot and bubbly. Serve.

(6 SERVINGS)

◆ Vegetables and Beans ◆

Basque Bean Casserole

Make this ahead of time, then reheat for a convenient meal.

1 lb	dried beans (Great Northern, Yellow Eye or Pinto)	450 g
4 cups	cold water	1 L
1/4 lb	unsliced bacon or salt pork	115 g
2	medium leeks, thinly sliced	2
2 cups	chopped onion	500 mL
1	medium whole onion	1
6	whole cloves	6
1 3/4 cups	canned chicken broth	425 mL
5	carrots, cut into 1-inch (2.5-cm) slices	5
3	cloves garlic, minced	3
2 tsp	Tabasco® pepper sauce	10 mL
1 tsp	dried thyme	5 mL
1 tsp	dried marjoram	5 mL
1 tsp	dried sage	5 mL
2	bay leaves	2
6	whole black peppercorns	6
2 cups	canned whole tomatoes, crushed	500 mL
1 lb	Polish sausage, cut into 1-inch (2.5-cm) slices	450 g

◆ Place beans and water in a 6-qt (6-L) oven-proof kettle or saucepot. Let soak 2 hours. Do not drain.

◆ Meanwhile, in a skillet over medium heat, brown bacon on both sides. Remove and drain on paper towels. Add leeks and chopped onion to skillet. Cook 10 minutes.

◆ Add bacon, leeks and onions to soaked beans.

◆ Stud whole onion with cloves. Add whole onion, chicken broth, carrots, garlic, Tabasco pepper sauce, thyme, marjoram, sage, bay leaves and peppercorns to beans. Bring to a boil. Cover, reduce heat and simmer 1 hour. Stir in tomatoes and sausage.

◆ Cover and bake at 350°F (180°C) 1 hour or until almost all liquid is absorbed. Serve.

(8 SERVINGS)

Irish Potato Champ

Special treatment for mashed potatoes.

1¹/₂ lbs	baking potatoes, peeled	675 g
6 tbsp	light olive oil	90 mL
¹/₂ tsp	Tabasco® pepper sauce	2 mL
1	clove garlic, peeled and minced	1
1	bunch green onions, chopped	1

◆ Place potatoes in a saucepan and fill with cold water. Bring to a boil over high heat. Reduce heat to medium and cook 20 to 25 minutes, or until potatoes are tender when pierced with a fork. Drain.

◆ Pass potatoes through a ricer or place in a bowl and mash with a potato masher. Cover and keep warm.

◆ In a small skillet over medium heat, combine olive oil, Tabasco pepper sauce, garlic and green onions. Sauté 1 to 2 minutes or until onions are slightly wilted. Stir into potatoes and serve immediately.

(6 SERVINGS)

Ratatouille

All the tastes of summer in a single dish.

1/3 cup	olive oil	75 mL
1/2 tsp	Tabasco® pepper sauce	2 mL
1	clove garlic, mashed	1
2	medium onions, thinly sliced	2
3	small zucchini, sliced	3
1	medium eggplant, pared and cubed	1
3	ripe tomatoes, coarsely chopped	3
1	large green pepper, cut in strips	1
1 tsp	salt	5 mL
1 tbsp	dried oregano	15 mL

◆ Heat olive oil in a large skillet. Add Tabasco pepper sauce, garlic and onion and cook until onion is tender, but not brown.

◆ Add remaining ingredients to skillet, one at a time, sprinkling with salt and oregano after each addition.

◆ Cover and cook over low heat 20 to 25 minutes, or until vegetables are tender, stirring occasionally. Serve immediately or chill and serve cold.

(6 SERVINGS)

◆ ◆

Honeyed Carrots

These carrots have great texture and a sweet spicy flavor.

1 lb	carrots, thinly sliced	450 g
1/4 cup	golden raisins	50 mL
2 tbsp	salted butter or margarine	30 mL
3 tbsp	honey	45 mL
1 tbsp	lemon juice	15 mL
1/4 tsp	ground ginger	1 mL
1/4 tsp	Tabasco® pepper sauce	1 mL
1/4 cup	sliced unpeeled almonds	50 mL

◆ Preheat oven to 375°F (190°C). Place carrots in a medium saucepan and cover with 1/2 inch (1 cm) of boiling water. Boil 8 minutes over medium heat; drain.

◆ Remove carrots to a 1-qt (1-L) baking dish. Stir in raisins, margarine, honey, lemon juice, ginger and Tabasco pepper sauce. Bake, uncovered, 25 to 30 minutes, stirring occasionally until carrots are glazed. Spoon into serving bowl and sprinkle with almonds.

(4 SERVINGS)

Piquant Onions

These onions are marvellous with beef or pork.

2 lbs	small white onions	900 g
1/4 cup	butter or margarine	50 mL
1 3/4 cups	canned beef broth (not condensed)	425 mL
1 cup	tomato sauce	250 mL
3 tbsp	cider vinegar	45 mL
2/3 cup	seedless dark raisins	150 mL
1 tbsp	sugar	15 mL
1/4 tsp	dried thyme, crumbled	1 mL
1/4 tsp	salt	1 mL
1	bay leaf	1
1 tbsp	water	15 mL
1 tbsp	cornstarch	15 mL
1/2 tsp	Tabasco® pepper sauce	2 mL

◆ Peel onions. Cut an "X" in stem ends to prevent onions from splitting.

◆ Heat butter in a 10-inch (25-cm) skillet; add onions and sauté until lightly browned.

◆ Add beef broth, tomato sauce, vinegar, raisins, sugar, thyme, salt and bay leaf. Cover and bring to a boil. Reduce heat, simmer 40 to 45 minutes or until onions are tender. Remove bay leaf.

◆ In a small cup, combine water and cornstarch. Stir into tomato mixture. Add Tabasco pepper sauce. Cook, stirring mixture until it boils and thickens. Serve.

(6 SERVINGS)

◆◆◆◆◆◆◆◆◆◆◆◆◆◆◆◆◆◆◆◆◆◆◆◆

Sausage Corn Tart

Serve this with a seasonal green salad for a great meal.

2 cups	fresh corn kernels	500 mL
1/2 lb	hot Italian sausage	225 g
1	small red pepper, diced	1
1	green onion, sliced	1
1	package prepared pie crust	1
3	large eggs	3
1 cup	milk	250 mL
1/4 cup	all-purpose flour	50 mL
1 tsp	Tabasco® pepper sauce	5 mL
1/2 tsp	dry mustard	2 mL
1/2 tsp	salt	2 mL

◆ In a 2-qt (2-L) saucepan, cover corn with water and bring to a boil. Reduce heat to low; cover and simmer 5 minutes until corn is tender. Drain.

◆ Remove casing from sausage. In a 10-inch (25-cm) skillet over medium heat, cook sausage until well- browned on all sides, stirring to crumble sausage. With slotted spoon, remove sausage to plate.

◆ In drippings remaining in skillet, cook red pepper 3 minutes; add green onion and cook 2 minutes, stirring occasionally.

◆ Preheat oven to 450°F (230°C). Line a 10-inch (25-cm) fluted tart pan* with removable bottom with prepared pie crust. Cover with wax paper and fill with uncooked rice. Bake 10 minutes. Remove rice and wax paper.

◆ In a large bowl, beat remaining ingredients together until well-blended. Stir in corn, sausage, red pepper and green onion. Spoon mixture into prepared pie crust.

◆ Lower oven to 350°F (180°C); bake 40 minutes or until knife inserted in center comes out clean.

* *Or, substitute a 9-inch (22-cm) pie plate for tart pan.*

(6 SERVINGS)

Cook sausage over medium heat until well-browned on all sides, stirring to crumble sausage.

Cook red pepper 3 minutes in skillet; add green onion and cook 2 minutes, stirring occasionally.

In a large bowl, beat remaining ingredients together until well-blended.

Stir corn into egg mixture.

Incorporate sausage, red pepper and green onion.

Spoon mixture into prepared pie crust.

White Beans Florentine

A quick vegetarian main dish.

4 cups	canned white kidney beans, drained and rinsed	1 L
2 tbsp	olive oil	30 mL
1	medium onion, diced	1
2	medium cloves garlic, minced	2
1 cup	reduced sodium chicken broth	250 mL
1¼ tsp	Tabasco® pepper sauce	6 mL
1	bay leaf	1
¾ tsp	salt	3 mL
½ tsp	rubbed sage	2 mL
2 cups	loosely packed spinach leaves, shredded	500 mL
1	small tomato, chopped	1

◆ Mash ½ cup (125 mL) white kidney beans; set aside.

◆ Heat olive oil in a 12-inch (30-cm) skillet over medium heat. Add onions, cook 5 minutes, stirring occasionally. Add garlic, cook 2 minutes.

◆ Add chicken broth, whole and mashed beans, Tabasco pepper sauce, bay leaf, salt and sage. Bring to a boil over high heat. Reduce heat to low; simmer 5 minutes to blend flavors, stirring occasionally.

◆ Stir in spinach leaves; cook 1 minute, until spinach begins to wilt. Garnish each serving with chopped tomato and serve.

(4 SERVINGS)

Salsa Topped Baked Potatoes

A spicy alternative to butter or sour cream.

4	**large baking potatoes**	4
2 tbsp	**olive oil**	30 mL
1	**large onion, diced**	1
1	**medium zucchini, diced**	1
1	**medium yellow squash, diced**	1
2	**large cloves garlic, minced**	2
2	**large ripe tomatoes, chopped**	2
1/4 cup	**fresh basil**	50 mL
2 tbsp	**red wine vinegar**	30 mL
1 1/2 tbsp	**Tabasco® garlic pepper sauce blend**	25 mL
1/2 tsp	**salt**	2 mL

◆ Preheat oven to 450°F (230°C). Place potatoes in shallow pan and bake 45 minutes or until tender.

◆ Meanwhile, heat oil in a 12-inch (30-cm) skillet over medium heat. Add onion and cook 5 minutes. Add zucchini, yellow squash and garlic; cook 3 minutes.

◆ Add tomatoes, basil, vinegar, Tabasco garlic pepper sauce blend and salt. Bring to a boil over high heat. Reduce heat to low; simmer uncovered 5 minutes to blend flavors, stirring occasionally. Keep warm until potatoes are ready.

◆ When potatoes are done, slash and top with salsa.

(4 SERVINGS)

◆◆◆◆◆◆◆◆◆◆◆◆◆◆◆◆◆◆◆◆◆◆◆◆◆◆

Savory Vegetable Tart

This is a great way to use cooked vegetables –
just substitute them for the parsnips and broccoli.

CRUST:

2 cups	all-purpose flour	500 mL
3/4 cup	butter or margarine, melted	175 mL
1 tsp	dried dill weed	5 mL
1/2 tsp	salt	2 mL

FILLING:

3 tbsp	olive oil	45 mL
8 oz	parsnips, peeled and thinly sliced	240 g
4 oz	broccoli florets	120 g
4 oz	mushrooms, thinly sliced	120 g
1	small leek, sliced and well-rinsed	1
1	small red bell pepper, seeded and cut into thin strips	1
1 tsp	salt	5 mL
1 cup	half-and-half cream	250 mL
1/2 cup	shredded cheddar cheese	125 mL
1	large egg	1
1 1/2 tsp	Tabasco® pepper sauce	7 mL

◆ Preheat oven to 375°F (190°C). In a large bowl, combine flour, butter, dill and salt. Press mixture into a fluted 9-inch (22-cm) tart pan with removable bottom or a 9-inch (22-cm) pie plate. Bake 10 minutes.

◆ Meanwhile, heat oil in a 12-inch (30-cm) skillet over medium heat. Add parsnips and broccoli and cook 3 minutes. Add mushrooms, leek, red pepper and salt; cook 7 minutes or until vegetables are tender-crisp.

◆ Combine cream, cheese, egg and Tabasco pepper sauce in a medium bowl. Spoon vegetables into crust and top with cheese mixture. Bake 35 to 40 minutes until knife inserted in the center of the pie comes out clean.

(6 SERVINGS)

◆◆◆◆◆◆◆◆◆◆◆◆◆◆◆◆◆◆◆◆◆◆◆◆

Grilled Vegetables al Fresco

Perfect with burgers, steak or chicken – easy too.

2	large red peppers	2
2	medium zucchini	2
1	large eggplant	1

SPICY MARINADE:

2/3 cup	white wine vinegar	150 mL
1/2 cup	soy sauce	125 mL
2 tbsp	minced ginger	30 mL
2 tbsp	olive oil	30 mL
2 tbsp	sesame oil	30 mL
2	large garlic cloves, minced	2
2 tsp	Tabasco® pepper sauce	10 mL

◆ Seed red peppers and cut into quarters. Cut each zucchini lengthwise into ¼-inch (5-mm) thick strips. Slice eggplant into ¼-inch (5-mm) thick rounds.

◆ In a 13 × 9-inch (32 × 22-cm) baking dish, combine Spicy Marinade ingredients. Place vegetable pieces in mixture; toss to mix well. Cover and refrigerate vegetables at least 2 hours and up to 24 hours, turning occasionally.

◆ About 30 minutes before serving, preheat grill to medium, placing rack 5-6 inches (12-15 cm) above coals.* Place red peppers, zucchini and eggplant slices on rack. Grill vegetables 4 minutes, turning once and brushing occasionally with marinade.

* *If using oven broiler, grill vegetables 5-6 inches (12-15 cm) below flame, 4 minutes on each side.*

(4 SERVINGS)

◆◆◆◆◆◆◆◆◆◆◆◆◆◆◆◆◆◆◆◆◆◆◆◆◆

Zucchini and Corn with Jalapeño Cream

A new way to cook zucchini and an excellent filling for vegetarian soft tacos.

2 tbsp	vegetable oil	30 mL
1/2 cup	chopped onion	125 mL
1	clove garlic, minced	1
6	small zucchini, cut into 1/2-inch (1-cm) cubes	6
1	10-oz (300-g) package frozen whole kernel corn, thawed	1
1/2 cup	"crema Mexicana" Mexican style whipping cream*	125 mL
1/2 lb	cheddar cheese, cut into 1/2-inch (1-cm) cubes	225 g
1/4 cup	finely chopped cilantro	50 mL
1 tsp	Tabasco® jalapeño sauce	5 mL
1/2 tsp	salt	2 mL

◆ Heat oil in a 12-inch (30-cm) skillet over medium-low heat. Add onion and garlic; cook until tender, about 2 minutes. Add zucchini; cook, stirring constantly, until zucchini is tender, about 5 minutes. Add corn; continue cooking 3 minutes. Reduce heat to low.

◆ Add "crema Mexicana", cheese pieces, cilantro, Tabasco jalapeño sauce and salt. Cook, uncovered, stirring gently, until thoroughly heated and cheese is melted. Serve immediately.

* *A mixture of 1/2 tsp (2 mL) flour with 1/2 cup (125 mL) sour cream may be substituted for "crema Mexicana".*

(6 SERVINGS)

◆ Sauces ◆

◆◆◆◆◆◆◆◆◆◆◆◆◆◆◆◆◆◆◆◆◆◆◆

Avocado Cilantro Salsa

A variation on guacamole.

2	**large avocados, halved and pitted**	2
4	**tomatillos,* husks removed, washed, and cut into quarters**	4
1 cup	**loosely packed cilantro, leaves only**	250 mL
¼ cup	**chopped onion**	50 mL
2 tsp	**Tabasco® jalapeño sauce**	10 mL
1 tsp	**salt**	5 mL

◆ Scoop avocados into the container of a blender or food processor. Add tomatillos, cilantro, onion, Tabasco jalapeño sauce and salt. Process until smooth.

◆ If not using immediately, cover with plastic wrap directly on top of salsa and refrigerate. Serve with tortilla chips for dipping.

* *Tomatillos, also known as Mexican green tomatoes, can be found in specialty produce stores. If they are not available, you can substitute 4 cherry tomatoes, quartered.*

(1½ CUPS – 375 ML)

Spicy Tomato Salsa

An ideal dip for tortilla chips.

1 cup	**finely diced, ripe fresh tomatoes**	250 mL
3 tbsp	**minced green onions**	45 mL
1 tbsp	**minced cilantro**	15 mL
1½ tsp	**freshly-squeezed lemon juice**	7 mL
¼ tsp	**ground cumin**	1 mL
⅛ tsp	**salt**	0.5 mL
1½ tsp	**Tabasco® garlic pepper sauce blend**	7 mL

◆ Combine all ingredients in a small bowl. Cover and refrigerate 1 to 2 hours to blend flavors.

(1 CUP – 250 ML)

◆ ◆

Fire and Ice Melon Salsa

A sweet and spicy combination perfect for chicken or ham.

1	large pineapple, peeled, cored and cut in 1/2-inch (1-cm) cubes	1
1 cup	granulated sugar	250 mL
2 tbsp	chopped fresh mint	30 mL
1/2 cup	apple cider vinegar	125 mL
3 oz	Tabasco® jalapeño sauce	85 mL
1/2	cantaloupe, peeled, seeded and cut in 1/2-inch (1-cm) cubes	1/2
1/2	honeydew melon, peeled, seeded and cut in 1/2-inch (1-cm) cubes	1/2

◆ Place pineapple, sugar, mint and vinegar in a saucepan and bring to a boil. Boil 5 minutes and reduce to low. Simmer 15 to 20 minutes or until mixture thickens into a syrup. Add Tabasco jalapeño sauce and simmer 5 minutes.

◆ Remove from heat, add melon and mix thoroughly. Refrigerate at least 4 hours before serving.

(6 CUPS – 1.5 L)

Piquante Sauce

Use as cocktail or dipping sauce for seafood.

2/3 cup	ketchup	150 mL
1/3 cup	chili sauce	75 mL
2 tbsp	capers	30 mL
2 tbsp	prepared horseradish	30 mL
2 tbsp	lemon juice	30 mL
1/2 tsp	Tabasco® pepper sauce	2 mL

◆ In a large bowl, stir together all ingredients until well blended.

(1 1/4 CUPS – 300 ML)

Salsa Verde

A superb sauce for chicken or pork.

1/4 cup	wine vinegar	50 mL	1/2 tsp	Tabasco® pepper sauce	2 mL
1/4 cup	olive oil	50 mL	1/2 tsp	garlic powder	2 mL
1 cup	parsley	250 mL		Pinch of sugar	
2 tbsp	capers	30 mL			
1	slice bread, crumbled	1			
1/2 tsp	salt	2 mL			

◆ Purée all ingredients 30 seconds with a blender or food processor. Serve with hot or cold chicken or pork.

(3/4 CUP – 175 ML)

Southern Style Grilling Sauce

A hearty sauce especially good with beef.

³/4 cup	ketchup	175 mL
¹/2 cup	cider vinegar	125 mL
¹/2 cup	brown sugar	125 mL
3 tbsp	Worcestershire sauce	45 mL
3 tbsp	vegetable oil	45 mL
2 tbsp	fresh lemon juice	30 mL
2 ¹/2 tbsp	chili powder	40 mL
2 tsp	Dijon mustard	10 mL
¹/2 tsp	Tabasco® pepper sauce	2 mL
¹/2 tsp	salt	2 mL
¹/2 tsp	freshly ground black pepper	2 mL
1	small onion, minced	1
2	cloves garlic, minced	2

◆ In a medium bowl, mix all ingredients and refrigerate overnight before serving.

(2 CUPS – 500 ML)

◆◆◆◆◆◆◆◆◆◆◆◆◆◆◆◆◆◆◆◆◆◆◆◆◆◆◆

Spicy Red Pepper Jelly

Spoon this over a block of cream cheese for a delicious appetizer.

5	**large red bell peppers, diced**	5
1	**small onion, cut into 6 pieces**	1
1½ cups	**apple cider vinegar**	375 mL
4 cups	**granulated sugar**	1 L
1	**3-oz (90-g) pouch liquid pectin**	1
1 tbsp	**Tabasco® pepper sauce**	15 mL

◆ Place bell peppers, onion and ¼ cup (50 mL) of vinegar in a food processor. Process until very finely ground.

◆ Scrape into a large, heavy non-aluminum pot. Add remaining vinegar and bring to a full boil over high heat. Reduce heat to low and simmer, stirring occasionally, until mixture is slightly thickened, about 5 minutes.

◆ Stir in sugar; raise heat to high and bring to a full rolling boil, stirring constantly.* Let boil 1 minute. Remove from heat.

◆ Stir in pectin and mix until completely blended. Skim off foam that rises to the surface. Stir in Tabasco pepper sauce.

◆ Ladle jam into hot sterilized jars, leaving ¼-inch (5-mm) headspace. Wipe the inside and outside rims clean with a damp paper towel. Seal with sterilized 2-piece lids, following manufacturer's instructions. Cool jars on wire rack.

◆ Store in a cool place up to 6 months. Once opened, keep refrigerated.

* *Be careful: jam has a tendency to boil over and is very hot. Reduce heat slightly, if necessary.*

(7 CUPS – 1.75 L)

Process bell peppers, onion and ¼ cup (50 mL) of vinegar until very finely ground.

Scrape into a large pot, add remaining vinegar and bring to a full boil over high heat.

Stir in sugar; raise heat to high and bring to a full rolling boil, stirring constantly.

Stir in pectin and mix until completely blended.

Skim off foam that rises to the surface.

Stir in Tabasco pepper sauce.

◆ ◆

Jamaican Barbecue Sauce

Easy island flavor.

1/3 cup	molasses	75 mL
1/3 cup	prepared mustard	75 mL
1/3 cup	red wine vinegar	75 mL
3 tbsp	Worcestershire sauce	45 mL
3/4 tsp	Tabasco® pepper sauce	3 mL

◆ Mix together all ingredients in a small bowl.

◆ Use as a baste for all kinds of meat on the grill, or serve on the side.

(1 CUP – 250 ML)

New Mexico Marinade

Beer lightens the flavor of this marinade for beef, pork or chicken.

1 1/2 cups	beer	375 mL
1/2 cup	chopped fresh cilantro	125 mL
3	large cloves garlic	3
1/2 cup	lime juice	125 mL
2 tsp	chili powder	10 mL
1 tsp	Tabasco® pepper sauce	5 mL
1 1/2 tsp	ground cumin	7 mL

◆ Mix all ingredients with a food processor or blender until well-combined.

◆ Marinade can be stored for up to 3 days in a covered jar in the refrigerator.

(2 1/2 CUPS – 625 ML)

Port Wine-Citrus Basting Sauce

Lovely deep flavor complements poultry and game.

1/2 cup	unsalted butter or margarine	125 mL
1 cup	brown sugar	250 mL
1/2 cup	orange juice	125 mL
	Juice of 1 lemon	
1/2 cup	port wine	125 mL
1/2 tsp	Tabasco® pepper sauce	2 mL
	Salt and pepper to taste	

◆ Melt butter in a medium, non-aluminum saucepan. Add remaining ingredients and cook until sugar is dissolved.

◆ Cool to room temperature before basting chicken, quail, duck or turkey.

(1 1/2 CUPS – 375 ML)

Southwestern Pasta Sauce

Tomato–cilantro sauce with real zip.

¹/₄ cup	olive oil	50 mL
2	medium onions, sliced	2
1	clove garlic, minced	1
3¹/₂ cups	canned tomatoes, crushed	875 mL
³/₄ tsp	Tabasco® pepper sauce	3 mL
¹/₄ tsp	salt	1 mL
2 tbsp	minced fresh cilantro	30 mL
¹/₄ tsp	granulated sugar	1 mL

◆ Heat oil over medium heat in large, heavy non-aluminum saucepan. Stir in onions and garlic; sauté, stirring occasionally, 10-12 minutes, or until tender.

◆ Add tomatoes, Tabasco pepper sauce, salt, cilantro and sugar; bring to a boil. Reduce heat to low and simmer, uncovered, 30 minutes until slightly thickened.

◆ Serve over hot pasta.

(4 SERVINGS)

◆ Poultry ◆

◆◆◆◆◆◆◆◆◆◆◆◆◆◆◆◆◆◆◆◆◆◆◆◆◆◆◆◆

Cornish Hens with Oyster Dressing

An elegant entrée for a dinner party.

3/4 cup	butter or margarine, divided	175 mL
1 cup	chopped onion	250 mL
1 cup	chopped celery	250 mL
1/2 cup	chopped shallots	125 mL
1/2 cup	chopped red bell pepper	125 mL
1/2 cup	chopped green bell pepper	125 mL
2	medium cloves garlic, minced	2
2	bay leaves	2
24	fresh oysters with liquid	24
3/4 tsp	dried thyme, crumbled	3 mL
1/2 tsp	dried oregano, crumbled	2 mL
3/4 tsp	Tabasco® pepper sauce	3 mL
5 cups	cooked rice	1.2 L
6	Cornish game hens	6
1/4 tsp	salt	1 mL
1 tbsp	all-purpose flour	15 mL
1 cup	chicken broth	250 mL

◆ Melt 1/2 cup (125 mL) butter in a large skillet; sauté onion, celery, shallots, red and green pepper, garlic and bay leaves 5 minutes.

◆ Chop oysters, reserving liquid, and stir oysters into skillet with 1/2 tsp (2 mL) thyme, oregano and 1/2 tsp (2 mL) Tabasco pepper sauce. Simmer 5 minutes. Remove bay leaves. Add rice and oyster liquid.

◆ Wash Cornish hens and pat dry. Stuff cavity of each hen with rice mixture. Set aside remaining stuffing.

◆ Preheat oven to 350°F (180°C). Arrange hens on rack in shallow roasting pan. Melt remaining 1/4 cup (50 mL) of butter in skillet; stir in salt, remaining 1/4 tsp (1 mL) thyme and 1/4 tsp (1 mL) Tabasco pepper sauce. Brush hens with butter mixture.

◆ Bake for 11/2 hours, basting frequently with drippings in pan. Bake reserved stuffing in a covered dish during last half hour of roasting time.

◆ When done, spoon extra stuffing on serving platter and arrange hens on top.

◆ To make gravy, pour out excess fat in roasting pan; add flour and stir. Place pan on stove over medium heat. Gradually add broth, scraping up bits from bottom of pan. Stir until mixture thickens and boils. Serve with hens.

(6 SERVINGS)

Roast Duck with Cumberland Sauce

The sweet-sour sauce complements the duck perfectly.

1	**4-lb (1.8-kg) duck**	1
1 tsp	**Tabasco® pepper sauce**	5 mL
	Salt	
¾ cup	**currant jelly**	175 mL
¾ cup	**orange juice**	175 mL
¼ cup	**lemon juice**	50 mL
¼ tsp	**ground ginger**	1 mL
1 tbsp	**cornstarch**	15 mL
2 tbsp	**water**	30 mL

◆ Preheat oven to 375°F (190°C). Pierce skin of duck with fork; rub with ½ tsp (2 mL) Tabasco pepper sauce and sprinkle with salt. Place on rack in roasting pan. Roast 1½ hours or until temperature of meat reaches 190°F (95°C).

◆ Meanwhile, melt jelly in a small saucepan over medium heat. Gradually stir in juices. Add ginger and remaining ½ tsp (2 mL) Tabasco pepper sauce.

◆ In a small bowl, dissolve cornstarch in water. Add to saucepan. Bring to a boil and boil 1 minute, stirring constantly. Serve with roast duck.

(4 SERVINGS)

Chicken Louisiana

A quick dish, excellent with cooked rice.

2 tbsp	vegetable oil	30 mL
1	large red bell pepper, cored and cut into thin strips	1
1	large green bell pepper, cored and cut into thin strips	1
6	boneless, skinless chicken breast halves	6
2 tbsp	all-purpose flour	30 mL
3/4 cup	chicken broth	175 mL
3/4 tsp	Tabasco® pepper sauce	3 mL
1/4 tsp	salt	1 mL

◆ Heat 1 tbsp (15 mL) of vegetable oil in a large skillet over medium heat. Add peppers and sauté about 5 minutes or until tender-crisp, stirring occasionally. With slotted spoon, remove peppers to platter.

◆ In the same skillet, heat remaining tbsp (15 mL) of oil over medium-high heat. Add chicken breasts; cook until well browned on both sides, about 5 minutes, turning once. Remove to platter with peppers.

◆ Stir flour into drippings remaining in skillet over medium heat. Cook, stirring constantly, until flour is dark brown but not burned. Gradually add chicken broth, Tabasco pepper sauce and salt. Cook until mixture thickens.

◆ Pour over chicken and serve.

(6 SERVINGS)

◆◆◆◆◆◆◆◆◆◆◆◆◆◆◆◆◆◆◆◆◆◆◆

Moroccan Chicken

An easy and exciting dish.

1 tbsp	olive oil	15 mL
8	chicken thighs	8
2	medium onions, quartered	2
1 cup	chicken broth	250 mL
1/3 cup	tomato paste	75 mL
1 tsp	salt	5 mL
3/4 tsp	ground ginger	3 mL
1/4 tsp	ground allspice	1 mL
2	medium carrots, cut into 1-inch (2.5-cm) chunks	2
2	medium zucchini, sliced 1/4-inch (5-mm) thick	2
1 cup	canned, drained chick peas	250 mL
1 tsp	Tabasco® pepper sauce	5 mL

◆ Heat oil in a heavy deep kettle over medium heat; add chicken thighs and brown on all sides. Add onions and cook 5 minutes until translucent. Add chicken broth and stir in tomato paste, salt, ginger and allspice. Cover and cook 10 minutes.

◆ Add carrots and simmer 10 minutes. Stir in zucchini, chick peas and Tabasco sauce. Cook, uncovered, stirring occasionally, until vegetables are tender, about 5 minutes. Serve with additional Tabasco pepper sauce, if desired.

(4 SERVINGS)

Spicy Baked Chicken

An easy dish with spirit.

1	3-lb (1.4-kg) broiler-fryer chicken, cut into pieces	1
1	chicken bouillon cube	1
1/2 cup	boiling water	125 mL
2 tsp	Worcestershire sauce	10 mL
2	cloves garlic, minced	2
1 tsp	curry powder	5 mL
1 tsp	dried oregano	5 mL
1 tsp	salt	5 mL
1/2 tsp	dry mustard	2 mL
1/2 tsp	paprika	2 mL
1 tsp	Tabasco® pepper sauce	5 mL

◆ Preheat oven to 375°F (190°C). Place chicken pieces, skin-side down, in a large shallow baking pan.

◆ In a measuring cup, dissolve bouillon cube in boiling water. Add remaining ingredients and mix well.

◆ Spoon mixture over chicken and bake 30 minutes. Turn chicken over; baste with juices in pan. Bake another 20 to 30 minutes or until chicken is done. Serve.

(4 SERVINGS)

◆◆◆◆◆◆◆◆◆◆◆◆◆◆◆◆◆◆◆◆◆◆◆◆◆◆◆

Chicken, Pork and Sausage Jambalaya

Louisiana's famous dish.

4 tbsp	vegetable oil	60 mL
3 lbs	broiler-fryer chicken parts	1.4 kg
½ lb	boneless pork, cut into thin strips	225 g
½ lb	andouille or smoked sausage, cut into ½-inch (1-cm) slices	225 g
1 cup	sliced celery	250 mL
1 cup	chopped onion	250 mL
1 cup	chopped green pepper	250 mL
1	clove garlic, minced	1
4 cups	canned whole peeled tomatoes, coarsely chopped and undrained	1 L
1 cup	chicken broth	250 mL
¾ cup	tomato paste	175 mL
1 tsp	Tabasco® pepper sauce	5 mL
1	bay leaf	1
½ tsp	salt	2 mL
1 tsp	dried oregano	5 mL
1 tsp	dried thyme	5 mL
½ tsp	ground allspice	2 mL
1½ cups	uncooked rice	375 mL

◆ Heat 2 tbsp (30 mL) of oil in a 5-qt (5-L) heavy kettle or saucepot over medium-high heat. Add chicken and brown on all sides, about 10 minutes. Remove.

◆ Heat remaining 2 tbsp (30 mL) of oil in saucepot. Add pork, sausage, celery, onion, green pepper and garlic, stirring frequently. Cook 8 to 10 minutes or until tender. Stir in all remaining ingredients except rice.

◆ Return chicken to saucepot. Cover, reduce heat and simmer 10 minutes. Stir in rice; cover. Simmer 40 minutes or until chicken and rice are tender, stirring frequently. Add additional broth if rice begins to stick to bottom of saucepot. Serve.

(8 SERVINGS)

Heat oil, add chicken and brown on all sides, about 10 minutes. Remove.

Heat remaining oil and add pork, sausage, celery, onion, green pepper and garlic, stirring frequently.

Stir in all remaining ingredients except rice.

Return chicken to saucepot. Cover, reduce heat and simmer 10 minutes.

Stir in rice; cover and simmer 40 minutes or until chicken and rice are tender, stirring frequently.

Chicken and Shrimp Mixed Grill

Serve each person a skewer of shrimp and half a chicken breast.

1 lb	**medium shrimp, peeled and deveined**	450 g
4	**boneless, skinless chicken breast halves**	4

SPICY MARINADE:

2/3 cup	**white wine vinegar**	150 mL
1/2 cup	**soy sauce**	125 mL
2 tbsp	**minced ginger**	30 mL
2 tbsp	**olive oil**	30 mL
2 tbsp	**sesame oil**	30 mL
2	**large cloves garlic, minced**	2
2 tbsp	**Tabasco® garlic pepper sauce blend**	30 mL
2	**green onions, sliced**	2

◆ Place shrimp on skewers. (If using wooden skewers, soak in water while preparing marinade.)

◆ Combine marinade ingredients in a 13 × 9-inch (32 × 22-cm) baking dish. Place skewered shrimp and chicken breasts in marinade; toss to mix well. Cover and refrigerate at least 2 hours and up to 24 hours, turning occasionally.

◆ About 30 minutes before serving, pre-heat grill to medium heat, placing rack 5 to 6 inches (12 to 15 cm) above coals.* Place skewered shrimp and chicken on rack. Grill shrimp 3 to 4 minutes; grill chicken breasts 6 minutes, turning once and brushing occasionally with marinade.

* *If using oven broiler, place skewered shrimp and chicken on broiler pan. Broil 4 inches (10 cm) from heat source as above.*

(4 SERVINGS)

Spicy Thai Chicken

A divine medley of flavors.

³/4 cup	canned cream of coconut	175 mL
3 tbsp	lime juice	45 mL
3 tbsp	soy sauce	45 mL
8	cilantro sprigs	8
3	large cloves garlic	3
3	large green onions, chopped	3
3	anchovy fillets	3
1 tbsp	Tabasco® garlic pepper sauce blend	15 mL
2	whole boneless, skinless chicken breasts, cut in half	2

◆ With a blender or food processor, combine cream of coconut, lime juice, soy sauce, cilantro, garlic, green onions, anchovies and Tabasco garlic pepper sauce blend. Cover and process until smooth.

◆ Place chicken in a large shallow dish; add marinade. Cover and refrigerate at least 2 hours, turning chicken occasionally.

◆ Remove chicken from marinade; place on grill about 5 inches (12 cm) from heat source. Brush generously with marinade. Grill 5 minutes. Turn chicken and brush with marinade. Grill 5 minutes or until chicken is cooked.

◆ Bring any remaining marinade to a boil and serve as dipping sauce with chicken.

(4 SERVINGS)

◆◆◆◆◆◆◆◆◆◆◆◆◆◆◆◆◆◆◆◆◆◆◆◆◆

Sautéed Chicken with Roasted Red Pepper Sauce

The roasted red peppers are well worth the effort.

3	large red bell peppers, cored and cut in half*	3
2 tsp	white wine vinegar	10 mL
1/2 tsp	Tabasco® pepper sauce	2 mL
1/4 tsp	salt	1 mL
3 tbsp	olive oil	45 mL
4	boneless chicken breast halves	4
	Salt and pepper	

◆ Place 4 pepper halves in a broiling pan. Baste with oil and broil about 5 minutes or until peppers are lightly charred. Remove peppers to bowl and cover with plastic wrap. Let peppers steam 10 minutes. Remove skin from peppers. Cut remaining uncooked pepper halves into slices and set aside.

◆ With a food processor or blender, combine roasted peppers, vinegar, Tabasco pepper sauce and salt. Gradually add 1 tbsp (15 mL) oil until mixture is smooth.

◆ Heat remaining oil in a heavy skillet over high heat. Sprinkle 4 pieces of chicken with salt and pepper and add them to the pan. Sauté 8-10 minutes on each side. Add sliced peppers to the pan and sauté 1-2 minutes. Serve with sauce.

* *Green or yellow peppers may be substituted.*

(4 SERVINGS)

Place 4 pepper halves in a broiling pan, baste with oil and broil about 5 minutes.

Remove peppers to bowl and cover with plastic wrap. Let peppers steam 10 minutes.

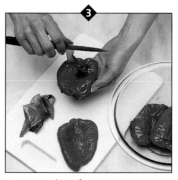

Remove skin from peppers.

With a food processor or blender, combine roasted peppers, vinegar, Tabasco pepper sauce and salt.

Gradually add 1 tbsp (15 mL) oil until mixture is smooth.

◆◆◆◆◆◆◆◆◆◆◆◆◆◆◆◆◆◆◆◆◆◆◆

Chicken Fajitas

Colorful and fun to eat.

2	**boneless, skinless chicken breasts**	2
2 tsp	**ground cumin**	10 mL
1½ tsp	**Tabasco® pepper sauce**	7 mL
1 tsp	**chili powder**	5 mL
½ tsp	**salt**	2 mL
8	**flour tortillas**	8
1 tbsp	**vegetable oil**	15 mL
3	**large green onions, cut into 2-inch (5-cm) pieces**	3

SPICY TOMATO SALSA:

1	**large ripe tomato, diced**	1
1 tbsp	**chopped cilantro**	15 mL
1 tbsp	**lime juice**	15 mL
¼ tsp	**Tabasco pepper sauce**	1 mL
¼ tsp	**salt**	1 mL

CORN RELISH:

1	**11-oz (330-g) can corn, drained**	1
½ cup	**diced green bell pepper**	125 mL
1 tbsp	**lime juice**	15 mL
¼ tsp	**Tabasco pepper sauce**	1 mL
¼ tsp	**salt**	1 mL

ACCOMPANIMENTS:

½ cup	**shredded cheddar cheese**	125 mL
½ cup	**sliced avocado**	125 mL
½ cup	**sour cream**	125 mL

◆ Cut chicken breasts into ½-inch (1-cm) strips. In a large bowl, toss chicken with cumin, Tabasco pepper sauce, chili powder and salt. Set aside.

◆ In a medium bowl, toss together salsa ingredients. In a separate bowl, toss together relish ingredients.

◆ Preheat oven to 350°F (180°C). Wrap tortillas in foil and warm 10 minutes in oven.

◆ Meanwhile, in a large skillet, heat vegetable oil over medium-high heat. Add chicken mixture; cook 4 minutes, stirring frequently. Add green onions; cook 1 minute or until chicken is browned and tender.

◆ Set out warmed tortillas with chicken, salsa, corn relish, cheddar cheese, avocados and sour cream. Place strips of chicken in center of each tortilla, add salsa, relish and toppings. Fold the bottom quarter and both sides of tortilla to cover filling.

(4 SERVINGS)

◆ ◆

Green Turkey Chili

Unusually light and delicious.

3 tbsp	olive oil	45 mL
3	large celery stalks, diced	3
1	large green bell pepper, seeded and diced	1
2	green onions, sliced	2
2	large cloves garlic, minced	2
1 lb	ground turkey	450 g
4 cups	canned white kidney beans, drained and rinsed	1 L
1/3 cup	Tabasco® jalapeño sauce	75 mL
1 1/2 cups	water	375 mL
1 1/4 tsp	salt	6 mL
1/4 cup	chopped parsley	50 mL

◆ Heat 2 tbsp (30 mL) of oil in a large saucepan over medium heat. Add celery and green pepper and cook 5 minutes. Add green onions and garlic; cook 5 minutes, stirring occasionally. With slotted spoon, remove vegetables to plate.

◆ Add remaining 1 tbsp (15 mL) oil. Over medium-high heat, cook ground turkey until well-browned on all sides, stirring frequently.

◆ Add cooked vegetables, kidney beans, Tabasco jalapeño sauce, water and salt. Bring to a boil over high heat; reduce heat to low. Cover and simmer 20 minutes, stirring occasionally. Uncover saucepan and simmer 5 minutes. Stir in parsley and serve.

(6 SERVINGS)

◆◆◆◆◆◆◆◆◆◆◆◆◆◆◆◆◆◆◆◆◆◆◆

One-pot Chicken Couscous

A simple version of a North African favorite.

¹/₄ cup	olive oil	50 mL
2 lbs	boneless, skinless chicken breasts, cut into 1-inch (2.5-cm) chunks	900 g
4	large carrots, peeled and sliced	4
2	medium onions, diced	2
2	large cloves garlic, minced	2
3¹/₂ cups	chicken broth	875 mL
2 cups	precooked couscous	500 mL
2 tsp	Tabasco® pepper sauce	10 mL
¹/₂ tsp	salt	2 mL
1 cup	raisins or currants	250 mL
1 cup	slivered almonds, toasted	250 mL
¹/₄ cup	fresh chopped parsley or mint	50 mL

◆ Heat oil in a 12-inch (30-cm) skillet over medium-high heat. Add chicken and cook until well-browned on all sides. With slotted spoon, remove chicken to plate.

◆ Reduce heat to medium. In drippings remaining in skillet, cook carrots and onion 5 minutes. Add garlic and cook 2 minutes, stirring frequently.

◆ Add chicken broth, couscous, Tabasco pepper sauce, salt and chicken. Bring to a boil, then reduce heat to low. Cover and simmer 5 minutes. Stir in raisins, almonds and parsley. Serve.

(8 SERVINGS)

◆ Meats ◆

Lamb Stew

Jalapeño sauce adds zing to a simple stew.

2 tbsp	vegetable oil	30 mL
1 lb	lamb for stew, cut into 3/4-inch (2-cm) pieces	450 g
4	large carrots, peeled and cut into 1/4-inch (5-mm) thick slices	4
4	medium all-purpose potatoes, peeled and diced	4
1	large onion, diced	1
1	large garlic clove, minced	1
2 cups	water	500 mL
1 tbsp	Tabasco® jalapeño sauce	15 mL
1 1/4 tsp	salt	6 mL
1 tbsp	all-purpose flour	15 mL
1 cup	frozen peas	250 mL
2 tbsp	chopped fresh parsley	30 mL

◆ Heat 1 tbsp (15 mL) of oil in a 4-qt (4-L) saucepot over medium-high heat. Add lamb and cook until well-browned on all sides, stirring occasionally. With slotted spoon, remove lamb to a bowl.

◆ Add remaining oil to drippings in skillet and cook carrots, potatoes, onion and garlic over medium heat until tender-crisp, about 10 minutes.

◆ Add water, Tabasco jalapeño sauce, salt and lamb to saucepot. Bring to a boil over high heat; reduce heat to low. Cover and simmer 25 minutes, stirring occasionally.

◆ In a small cup, combine flour and 2 tbsp (30 mL) water. Add to lamb mixture along with peas and parsley. Bring to a boil over high heat. Reduce heat to low, cover and simmer 5 minutes or until lamb and vegetables are tender. Serve.

(4 SERVINGS)

Ginger Marinated Flank Steak

Steak marinade with distinctive flavor and texture.

1	small onion, chopped	1
1	small carrot, sliced	1
1/2	rib celery, sliced	1/2
2	cloves garlic, chopped	2
1 tsp	chopped fresh ginger	5 mL
1/2 cup	rice wine vinegar	125 mL
1/4 cup	sesame oil	50 mL
1/2 tsp	salt	2 mL
1 tbsp	Tabasco® garlic pepper sauce blend	15 mL
2 1/2 lbs	whole flank steak, trimmed	1.2 kg

◆ With a blender or food processor, combine onion, carrot, celery, garlic and ginger; process into a smooth paste. Add vinegar, oil, salt and Tabasco garlic pepper sauce blend; process 2 minutes.

◆ Lightly score both sides of steak and place in a shallow baking dish. Pour marinade over steak. Cover and refrigerate 6 to 8 hours or overnight.

◆ Grill or broil steak, coated with marinade, over medium heat 3 to 4 minutes on each side or until center is medium-rare. Slice thinly on the diagonal and serve.

(8 SERVINGS)

Pork Chops with Apples and Bourbon

The sauce makes the dish.

4	boneless loin pork chops, trimmed and cut 1-inch (2.5-cm) thick	4
1	clove garlic, halved lengthwise	1
	Pinch of sage	
2 tbsp	margarine or unsalted butter	30 mL
1/2 tsp	Tabasco® pepper sauce	2 mL
1 tsp	fresh lemon juice	5 mL
1/2 cup	chopped onion	125 mL
1	medium Granny Smith apple, peeled and diced	1
1/3 cup	bourbon or apple cider	75 mL

◆ Pat pork chops dry. Rub chops on both sides with the cut sides of the garlic clove. Sprinkle with sage.

◆ In a large skillet over medium-high heat, combine margarine and Tabasco pepper sauce and heat until mixture sizzles. Add pork and sauté 10 to 14 minutes, turning once, or until chops are golden-brown on both sides and cooked through. Remove from pan, sprinkle with lemon juice and keep warm.

◆ Add onion to skillet and sauté 1 minute over medium heat. Stir in apple and sauté 1 minute. Add bourbon and cook 1 minute, stirring constantly. Spoon onion sauce over pork chops and serve.

(4 SERVINGS)

◆◆◆◆◆◆◆◆◆◆◆◆◆◆◆◆◆◆◆◆◆◆◆◆

Hungarian Beef Pot Pie

Caraway and paprika provide distinctive flavor.

¹/₄ lb	bacon, chopped	115 g
2 lbs	beef for stew, cut into 1-inch (2.5-cm) cubes	900 g
¹/₃ cup	all-purpose flour	75 mL
1	large onion, chopped	1
3	cloves garlic, minced	3
³/₄ lb	rutabaga, peeled, and cut into 1-inch (2.5-cm) cubes	350 g
2 cups	beef bouillon	500 mL
2 tbsp	paprika	30 mL
2	bay leaves	2
1 tsp	caraway seeds	5 mL
1 tsp	Tabasco® pepper sauce	5 mL
¹/₄ tsp	salt	1 mL
	Pastry for single crust 9-inch (22-cm) pie	

◆ Cook bacon in a large saucepan or heavy deep kettle; remove and set aside. Coat beef cubes with flour. Add to skillet, sauté meat in bacon fat until evenly-browned on all sides.

◆ Add onion and garlic; sauté until tender-crisp. Add rutabaga, bouillon, bacon, paprika, bay leaves, caraway seeds, Tabasco pepper sauce and salt. Cover and simmer 35 to 40 minutes, stirring occasionally. Spoon into a 2-qt (2-L) shallow baking dish.

◆ Preheat oven to 400°F (200°C). On a lightly floured board, roll out pastry ¹/₈-inch (2.5-mm) thick and 2 inches (5 cm) larger than baking dish.

◆ Place pastry over meat mixture. Fold excess pastry under, so that it is even with edge of baking dish. Flute edge. With a sharp knife, cut air vents in pastry. Bake 15 minutes until crust is golden brown. Serve.

(6 SERVINGS)

◆◆◆◆◆◆◆◆◆◆◆◆◆◆◆◆◆◆◆◆◆◆

Carnitas with Pico de Gallo

Long cooking brings out the best in the pork.

2 lbs	boneless pork shoulder, cut into 3/4-inch (2-cm) cubes	900 g
	Zest (colored rind only) of one lime, removed with a vegetable peeler	
2	cloves garlic	2
1 1/2 tbsp	Tabasco® garlic pepper sauce blend	25 mL
1/2 tsp	ground cumin	2 mL
1/2 tsp	salt	2 mL
12	corn tortillas	12

PICO DE GALLO:

1	large tomato, seeded and diced	1
1/2 cup	chopped onion	125 mL
1/2 cup	chopped cilantro, leaves only	125 mL
1	clove garlic, minced	1
1 1/2 tsp	Tabasco® garlic pepper sauce blend	7 mL
1/2	large avocado, peeled, seeded and diced	1/2
1 tsp	salt	5 mL

◆ In a 5-qt (5-L) heavy deep kettle, place pork, lime peel, garlic, Tabasco garlic pepper sauce blend and cumin; add water to barely cover. Bring to a boil. Reduce heat to low, cover and cook 2 1/2 hours, or until water has evaporated.

◆ Add salt and continue cooking pork in its own juice until browned. Remove lime zest and garlic. Drain off all excess fat. Adjust seasonings with salt and Tabasco garlic pepper sauce blend.

◆ Seal tortillas in a plastic bag. Microwave 1 minute on high. Carefully open bag allowing steam to escape. Remove tortillas from plastic bag and wrap in a kitchen towel to keep warm.

◆ Prepare Pico de Gallo: In a medium bowl, combine tomato, onion, cilantro, garlic and Tabasco garlic pepper sauce blend; toss to mix well. Just before serving, add avocado, salt and additional Tabasco garlic pepper sauce blend, if desired.

◆ Serve carnitas with warmed tortillas and Pico de Gallo. Place cooked pork in the center of each tortilla; add Pico de Gallo, then fold both sides of tortilla to cover filling.

(6 SERVINGS)

Place pork, lime peel, garlic, Tabasco garlic pepper sauce blend and cumin in a deep kettle; add water to barely cover.

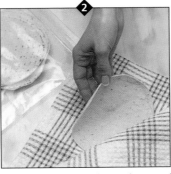

Seal tortillas in plastic bag and microwave 1 minute on high. Remove tortillas and wrap in a kitchen towel to keep warm.

Place cooked pork in the center of each tortilla; add Pico de Gallo, then fold both sides of tortilla to cover filling.

Chuckwagon Pot Roast

Tequila and Tabasco pepper sauce liven it up.

2	bacon slices	2
1	carrot, peeled and diced	1
1	onion, diced	1
3 lbs	beef chuck roast	1.4 kg
3 tbsp	all-purpose flour	45 mL
3 tbsp	tomato paste	45 mL
2 tbsp	tequila	30 mL
2	beef bouillon cubes	2
2 cups	red wine	500 mL
1 tbsp	Tabasco® pepper sauce	15 mL
2	bay leaves	2
1 tbsp	salt	15 mL

◆ In a heavy deep kettle, sauté bacon and add carrot and onion. Cook 2 minutes. Remove bacon and crumble; set aside with vegetables.

◆ Coat the roast with flour and brown on all sides in bacon fat.

◆ Add cooked vegetables, bacon and remaining ingredients. Bring sauce to a boil. Cover and simmer on medium-low heat 2 hours or until tender.

◆ When done, slice meat, pour sauce over slices and serve.

(6 SERVINGS)

Pork Saté

Captures the sweet, spicy Thai taste.

2 lbs	pork tenderloin, cut into 1-inch (2.5-cm) cubes	900 g
3/4 cup	creamy peanut butter	175 mL
1/2 cup	soy sauce	125 mL
1/4 cup	lime juice	50 mL
3 tbsp	brown sugar	45 mL
1 cup	chopped onion	250 mL
1 tbsp	ground coriander	15 mL
1 tbsp	Tabasco® garlic pepper sauce blend	15 mL

◆ Combine all ingredients in a large container with tight-fitting lid. Cover and marinate in refrigerator at least 3 hours.

◆ Thread about 5 pieces of meat on each of 8 skewers. Place on grill when coals have reached the light grey ash stage. Cook 10 minutes, turn and cook 10 minutes.

◆ Meanwhile, pour marinade into a saucepan, bring to a boil, lower heat and simmer for about 10 minutes, or until sauce is reduced and thickened. Serve on the side with pork Saté.

(8 SERVINGS)

◆◆◆◆◆◆◆◆◆◆◆◆◆◆◆◆◆◆◆◆◆◆◆◆

Venison Ragoût with Parsley Biscuits

A wholesome dish, rich in flavor.

4 oz	bacon, diced	120 g
1 lb	venison shoulder, cut into 1-inch (2.5-cm) chunks	450 g
3	large carrots, peeled and cut into ½-inch (1-cm) slices	3
3	large parsnips, peeled and cut into ½-inch (1-cm) slices	3
1 cup	pearl onions	250 mL
1 tbsp	butter or margarine	15 mL
6 oz	mushrooms, cut in half	180 g
2	cloves garlic, minced	2
1 cup	red wine	250 mL
1 tbsp	cornstarch	15 mL
1 cup	water	250 mL
2 tbsp	chopped fresh parsley, optional	30 mL
1 tbsp	tomato paste	15 mL
1 tsp	salt	5 mL
1 tsp	Tabasco® pepper sauce	5 mL
½ tsp	dried thyme	2 mL

◆ Cook bacon in a 12-inch (30-cm) skillet over medium heat, until crisp, stirring occasionally. With slotted spoon, remove to bowl. In drippings remaining in skillet, cook venison chunks over medium-high heat until well-browned on all sides, stirring frequently. With slotted spoon, remove to bowl with bacon.

◆ In same skillet, cook carrots, parsnips and onions about 5 minutes over medium heat. Add butter, mushrooms and garlic; cook 5 minutes or until vegetables are tender-crisp, stirring occasionally.

◆ Preheat oven to 350°F (180°C). Dissolve cornstarch in red wine. Add wine, bacon, venison and remaining ingredients to skillet. Bring to a boil over high heat. Spoon mixture into a 2-qt (2-L) shallow casserole. Cover with foil and bake 30 minutes.

◆ Meanwhile, prepare Parsley Biscuits.

◆ Remove casserole from oven and carefully remove lid. Increase oven to 450°F (230°C). Drop ⅓ cup (75 mL) of dough per biscuit onto mixture in casserole to make 6 biscuits. Bake 12 to 15 minutes until biscuits are golden. Serve with tossed green salad.

(6 SERVINGS)

Cook bacon in a 12-inch (30-cm) skillet over medium heat, until crisp, stirring occasionally.

Cook venison chunks in bacon drippings over medium-high heat until well-browned on all sides, stirring frequently.

In same skillet, cook carrots, parsnips and onions about 5 minutes over medium heat.

Parsley Biscuit Batter

2 cups	all-purpose flour	500 mL
1 tbsp	baking powder	15 mL
1/2 tsp	baking soda	2 mL
1/2 tsp	salt	2 mL
1/4 cup	butter or margarine, cut into small pieces	50 mL
1 cup	buttermilk	250 mL
3 tbsp	chopped fresh parsley	45 mL

◆ Combine flour, baking powder, baking soda and salt in a medium bowl. With pastry blender, cut butter into flour mixture until mixture resembles coarse crumbs. Add buttermilk and parsley; stir to moisten.

(6 BISCUITS)

Add butter, mushrooms and garlic; cook 5 minutes or until vegetables are tender-crisp.

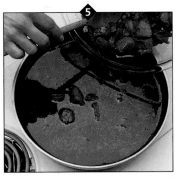

Add wine, bacon, venison and remaining ingredients to skillet. Bring to a boil over high heat.

Drop 1/3 cup (75 mL) of dough per parsley biscuit onto mixture in casserole to make 6 biscuits.

◆◆◆◆◆◆◆◆◆◆◆◆◆◆◆◆◆◆◆◆◆

Mustard Marinated Steak

Sure to become a cookout favorite.

1/2 cup	**Dijon mustard**	125 mL
3 tbsp	**soy sauce**	45 mL
3 tbsp	**dry sherry**	45 mL
2 tbsp	**brown sugar**	30 mL
1 tbsp	**vegetable oil**	15 mL
1	**clove garlic, minced**	1
1/2 tsp	**Tabasco® pepper sauce**	2 mL
2 lbs	**round steak, 1 1/2-inch (3.5-cm) thick**	900 g

◆ In a medium bowl, combine all ingredients except meat. Mix well. Place steak in a large shallow dish and add marinade. Cover and refrigerate at least 5 hours; turn meat occasionally.

◆ Remove meat from marinade, place on grill about 5 inches (12 cm) from heat source. Brush with marinade and grill 15 minutes. Turn meat, brush with marinade and grill 10 minutes or until cooked as desired.

◆ While meat is cooking, heat leftover marinade in a saucepan. Bring to a boil and reduce heat; simmer 2-3 minutes.

◆ Carve meat in thin slices against the grain. Drizzle some of marinade on the slices and serve.

(8 SERVINGS)

Tamale Pie

Long slow cooking brings out the flavor.

4 tbsp	**butter or margarine**	60 mL
1 1/2 lbs	**veal shoulder, cut into 1 1/2-inch (3.5-cm) cubes**	675 g
1	**small onion, chopped**	1
2	**cloves garlic, minced**	2
2	**eggs**	2
3/4 cup	**milk**	175 mL
1 tbsp	**Tabasco® garlic pepper sauce blend**	15 mL
1/2 cup	**cornmeal**	125 mL
2 cups	**canned stewed tomatoes, drained**	500 mL
2 cups	**canned cream style corn**	500 mL
12	**small pitted ripe olives**	12
2 tsp	**salt**	10 mL

◆ Melt butter in skillet. Add veal, onion and garlic; cook over low heat 15 minutes, stirring occasionally. Remove to a 13 × 9-inch (32 × 22-cm) baking dish.

◆ Combine eggs, milk and Tabasco garlic pepper sauce blend; stir in remaining ingredients. Pour on top of veal mixture.

◆ Place baking dish containing tamale pie into a larger baking pan. Pour boiling water into the pan so that it reaches about 1 inch (2.5 cm) below the top of the pie. Bake at 325°F (160°C) 1 1/2 hours, or until set.

(6 SERVINGS)

◆◆◆◆◆◆◆◆◆◆◆◆◆◆◆◆◆◆◆◆◆◆◆◆◆◆◆◆◆◆

Stuffed Cabbage Rolls
with Yogurt Dill Sauce

These plump packets are a real treat.

1	3-lb (1.4-kg) head green cabbage, cored	1
2 tbsp	olive oil	30 mL
3	large green onions, sliced	3
2	large cloves garlic, minced	2
1 lb	ground lamb	450 g
2 cups	plain yogurt	500 mL
4 tbsp	fresh snipped dill	60 mL
1½ tsp	Tabasco® pepper sauce	7 mL
1½ tsp	salt	7 mL

◆ Bring a large pot of water to a boil over high heat. Add cabbage, core-end down. Reduce heat to medium; cover and simmer 10-12 minutes, or until leaves are softened. Remove cabbage to bowl of cold water.

◆ Separate 16 large leaves and trim the tough ribs on the back so that they will roll up easily. Chop enough remaining cabbage to make 3 cups (750 mL).

◆ Heat oil in a 12-inch (30-cm) skillet over medium heat. Add chopped cabbage, green onions and garlic. Cook until tender, about 10 minutes, stirring occasionally. With slotted spoon, remove to bowl.

◆ Cook ground lamb in drippings remaining in skillet over high heat, stirring frequently, until well-browned on all sides. Remove to bowl with cabbage.

◆ In a food processor, blend lamb mixture until finely ground. In a large bowl, toss lamb mixture with ½ cup (125 mL) yogurt, 2 tbsp (30 mL) dill, Tabasco pepper sauce and salt; mix well. Place 3 tbsp (45 mL) lamb mixture at bottom of cabbage leaf and roll up tightly to form a 3-inch (8-cm) long roll, tucking ends in as you roll. Repeat with remaining lamb and leaves.

◆ Preheat oven to 400°F (200°C). Place cabbage rolls on rack in a roasting pan. Add 1 cup (250 mL) boiling water; cover pan tightly with foil. Bake 20 minutes.

◆ Meanwhile, in a medium bowl, combine remaining 1½ cups (375 mL) yogurt and 2 tbsp (30 mL) dill. When cabbage rolls are hot, remove to platter. Top with yogurt-dill sauce and serve.

(4-6 SERVINGS)

Place cabbage core-end down in a large pot of boiling water. Reduce heat to medium; cover and simmer 10-12 minutes.

Separate 16 large leaves and trim the tough ribs on the back so that they will roll up easily.

Place lamb mixture at bottom of cabbage leaf and roll up tightly to form a long roll, tucking ends in as you roll.

◆◆◆◆◆◆◆◆◆◆◆◆◆◆◆◆◆◆◆◆◆◆◆◆◆◆◆◆

Pork Loin with Sweet Onion Crust

A sensational way to roast pork.

2	large onions, thinly sliced	2
3 tbsp	olive oil	45 mL
1½ tsp	minced fresh rosemary leaves, or ¾ tsp (3 mL) dried rosemary, crushed	7 mL
1¼ tsp	Tabasco® pepper sauce	6 mL
1	clove garlic, minced	1
½ tsp	salt	2 mL
⅛ tsp	ground cloves	0.5 mL
1	3-lb (1.4-kg) boneless pork loin roast, trimmed of all visible fat and tied	1
1½ tbsp	dry white wine	25 mL
2 tbsp	plain dry bread crumbs	30 mL

◆ Place onions, 1 tbsp (15 mL) olive oil, rosemary, 1 tsp (5 mL) Tabasco pepper sauce, garlic, salt and cloves in a 9-inch (22-cm) baking dish. Mix well.

◆ Place pork loin in dish and coat with onion mixture. Cover and marinate in refrigerator at least 2 hours or overnight.

◆ Remove pork from onions and set aside. Heat 1 tbsp (15 mL) oil in a large non-stick skillet over high heat. Add onion marinade and sauté 1 minute. Reduce heat to medium-low and cook 12-15 minutes, stirring frequently, until onions are golden brown and very tender (add 1 tbsp (15 mL) of water if skillet gets too dry). Add wine and simmer until evaporated. Remove from heat.

◆ Add bread crumbs and remaining ¼ tsp (1 mL) Tabasco pepper sauce to onions and toss to mix well. Let cool.

◆ Preheat oven to 325°F (160°C). Meanwhile, heat remaining 1 tbsp (15 mL) of oil in a medium-size skillet. Add pork loin and cook about 4 minutes, turning to brown on all sides.

◆ Rinse and dry the baking dish used for marinating pork and grease it lightly. Transfer pork to dish and press onion mixture firmly on top and sides of pork. Roast pork about 1½ hours, until a meat thermometer inserted in the thickest part registers 150°F (75°C).

◆ Let pork stand 10 minutes. Carefully remove strings. Slice and serve.

(4-6 SERVINGS)

◆◆◆◆◆◆◆◆◆◆◆◆◆◆◆◆◆◆◆◆◆◆◆

Indonesian Lamb

Open up the spice cupboard for this one.

1½ tbsp	peanut or vegetable oil	25 mL
2 lbs	boneless lamb, trimmed of visible fat and cut into 1-inch (2.5-cm) cubes	900 g
2 tbsp	finely chopped onion	30 mL
2	cloves garlic, minced	2
1½ tbsp	Tabasco® garlic pepper sauce blend	25 mL
1 tsp	salt	5 mL
1 tsp	ground coriander	5 mL
½ tsp	grated lemon peel	2 mL
½ tsp	ground cinnamon	2 mL
¼ tsp	ground cumin	1 mL
¼ tsp	ground ginger	1 mL
¼ tsp	ground nutmeg	1 mL
⅛ tsp	ground cloves	0.5 mL
⅛ tsp	turmeric	0.5 mL
1 cup	beef broth	250 mL
½ cup	canned cream of coconut	125 mL

◆ Heat oil in a large skillet. Add meat and brown on all sides over high heat. Reduce heat to medium. Add onion, garlic, Tabasco garlic pepper sauce blend, salt, coriander, lemon peel, and all spices. Cook until onion is tender.

◆ Stir in beef broth and cream of coconut. Simmer 1 hour, or until meat is tender, stirring occasionally. Serve over cooked rice, if desired.

(6 SERVINGS)

◆◆◆◆◆◆◆◆◆◆◆◆◆◆◆◆◆◆◆◆◆◆◆◆◆

Three-Pepper Sausage Sauté

A colorful, flavorful dish.

1 lb	hot Italian sausages	450 g
1	large red bell pepper, cored	1
1	large green bell pepper, cored	1
1	large yellow bell pepper, cored	1
1	medium onion	1
1 tsp	dried oregano	5 mL
3/4 tsp	Tabasco® pepper sauce	3 mL
1/2 tsp	salt	2 mL
1/4 cup	water	50 mL

◆ In a 12-inch (30-cm) skillet over medium heat, cook sausages 15 minutes, or until browned on all sides, turning occasionally and pricking with a fork.

◆ Meanwhile, cut peppers into 1/2-inch (1-cm) thick slices. Cut onion in half and cut each half into 1/2-inch (1-cm) thick slices.

◆ Remove sausages to cutting board. In drippings remaining in skillet, cook peppers and onion about 5 minutes, stirring occasionally.

◆ When sausages are cool enough to handle, cut into 1-inch (2.5-cm) thick slices. Stir into skillet with oregano, Tabasco pepper sauce, salt and water. Bring to a boil and reduce heat to low. Cover, simmer 5 minutes to blend flavors, and serve.

(4 SERVINGS)

◆◆◆◆◆◆◆◆◆◆◆◆◆◆◆◆◆◆◆◆◆◆◆◆◆◆

Savory Venison Chili

A delicious way to serve lesser cuts of venison.

4 oz	bacon, diced	120 g
1	large onion, coarsely chopped	1
1	medium green bell pepper, seeded and cut into 3/4-inch (2-cm) chunks	1
1 lb	venison shoulder, cut into 1-inch (2.5-cm) chunks	450 g
1 tbsp	chili powder	15 mL
1 1/2 tsp	ground cumin	7 mL
3 1/2 cups	canned crushed tomatoes	875 mL
4 cups	canned red kidney beans, drained and rinsed	1 L
1/2 cup	water	125 mL
1 tbsp	Tabasco® pepper sauce	15 mL
1 1/2 tsp	salt	7 mL

◆ In a 5-qt (5-L) saucepot over medium heat, cook diced bacon until crisp. With slotted spoon, remove to a medium bowl.

◆ In drippings remaining in skillet, cook onion and green pepper until tender, stirring occasionally. With slotted spoon, remove to bowl with bacon.

◆ In same skillet over medium-high heat, cook venison in drippings until browned on all sides, stirring occasionally. Stir in chili powder and cumin; cook 1 minute.

◆ Add crushed tomatoes, red kidney beans, water, Tabasco pepper sauce, salt, bacon and vegetables. Bring to a boil over high heat. Reduce heat to low; cover and simmer 20 minutes or until venison is tender, stirring occasionally. Serve with garlic bread.

(8 SERVINGS)

Simmer veal, water, salt, thyme, bayleaf and parsley sprig 1 hour or until meat is tender.

Add onions and carrots; cook until vegetables are tender.

Drain stock into a large measuring cup and add water, if necessary, to make 2 cups (500 mL).

Blanquette de Veau

A lovely lemony stew.

1½ lbs	veal shoulder, cut into 1¼-inch (3-cm) cubes	675 g
4 cups	water	1 L
2 tsp	salt	10 mL
⅛ tsp	ground thyme	0.5 mL
1	bay leaf	1
1	fresh parsley sprig	1
12	small white onions, peeled	12
6	carrots, pared and quartered	6
2 tbsp	butter or margarine	30 mL
2 tbsp	all-purpose flour	30 mL
2	egg yolks	2
2 tbsp	lemon juice	30 mL
½ tsp	Tabasco® pepper sauce	2 mL
1 tbsp	finely chopped fresh parsley	15 mL

◆ In a deep saucepan, place veal, water, salt, thyme, bayleaf and parsley sprig; simmer over low heat 1 hour or until meat is tender.

◆ Add onions and carrots; cook until vegetables are tender. Drain stock into a large measuring cup and add water, if necessary, to make 2 cups (500 mL).

◆ Melt butter in a separate saucepan over medium heat. Blend in flour and slowly stir in stock. Cook, stirring constantly, until mixture thickens and boils.

◆ In a small bowl, combine egg yolks, lemon juice and Tabasco pepper sauce, beating lightly. Add about 1 cup (250 mL) of the hot sauce, stirring constantly, then stir mixture into the remaining sauce in saucepan. Stir over low heat until slightly thickened, but do not boil.

◆ Add sauce to veal and vegetables. Remove to serving bowl or platter and sprinkle with chopped parsley. Serve with hot cooked rice or noodles.

(6 SERVINGS)

Gradually add stock to butter and flour and cook, stirring constantly, until mixture thickens and boils.

Add egg yolk and sauce mixture to the remaining sauce. Stir over low heat until slightly thickened, but do not boil.

Add sauce to veal and vegetables.

◆ Fish and Seafood ◆

◆◆◆◆◆◆◆◆◆◆◆◆◆◆◆◆◆◆◆◆◆◆◆◆◆◆◆◆◆

Poached Salmon with Yogurt Dill Sauce

An elegant dish that's ready in 30 minutes.

2 cups	water	500 mL
1 cup	dry white wine or bottled clam juice	250 mL
1	lemon, sliced	1
1	small onion, sliced (optional)	1
2	bay leaves	2
8	black peppercorns	8
4	dill sprigs	4
1 tsp	Tabasco® pepper sauce	5 mL
1/4 tsp	salt	1 mL
4	8-oz (240-g) salmon steaks*	4

YOGURT DILL SAUCE:

1 cup	plain yogurt	250 mL
1 tbsp	chopped fresh dill	15 mL
1 tbsp	Dijon mustard	15 mL
1 tsp	lemon juice	5 mL
1/2 tsp	Tabasco pepper sauce	2 mL

◆ In a large skillet, combine water, wine, lemon, onion, bay leaves, peppercorns, dill, Tabasco pepper sauce and salt. Bring to a boil. Reduce heat to low, cover and simmer 15 minutes.

◆ Meanwhile, combine Yogurt Dill Sauce ingredients in a small bowl. Mix well.

◆ Add salmon to skillet. Cover and simmer 12 to 15 minutes or until fish flakes easily when tested with fork. Serve salmon steaks warm or chilled with Yogurt Dill Sauce.

* *This recipe also works well with halibut steaks.*

(4 SERVINGS)

◆◆◆◆◆◆◆◆◆◆◆◆◆◆◆◆◆◆◆◆◆◆◆◆◆

Brazilian Seafood Stew

A savory stew with nuances of coconut and cilantro.

3/4 lb	fish fillets (cod, striped bass, and snapper) cut in bite-size pieces	350 g
1 lb	medium shrimp, shelled and deveined	450 g
4 tbsp	lime juice	60 mL
1 1/2 tsp	Tabasco® pepper sauce	7 mL
1 tsp	salt	5 mL
2 tbsp	olive oil	30 mL
1 cup	chopped onion	250 mL
1 cup	chopped green bell pepper	250 mL
2	large cloves garlic, minced	2
4 cups	canned peeled whole tomatoes, undrained	1 L
3/4 cup	coconut milk*	175 mL
1 cup	chopped green onion	250 mL
1 cup	chopped fresh cilantro	250 mL
	Hot cooked rice	

◆ In a shallow non-aluminum bowl, combine fish, shrimp, 2 tbsp (30 mL) lime juice, 1/4 tsp (1 mL) Tabasco pepper sauce and 1/2 tsp (2 mL) salt; toss to mix. Cover and marinate in refrigerator 30 minutes.

◆ Heat oil in a large skillet over medium-high heat. Sauté onion, green pepper and garlic until tender. Break up tomatoes and add to skillet. Incorporate coconut milk, remaining 2 tbsp (30 mL) lime juice, 1 tsp (5 mL) Tabasco pepper sauce and 1/2 tsp (2 mL) salt. Mix well. Bring to a boil, reduce heat and simmer 2 to 3 minutes.

◆ Add marinated fish and simmer 10 minutes or until cooked through. Add shrimp and simmer 5 minutes. Just before serving, stir in green onion and cilantro. Serve over rice.

* *Coconut milk can be purchased in specialty stores or combine 1 cup (250 mL) shredded fresh coconut or packaged sweetened flaked coconut and 1 cup (250 mL) warm water in a blender or food processor. Process 40 seconds. Strain the mixture through a fine sieve in heavy cheese cloth, squeezing to remove all liquid from the coconut.*

(10 SERVINGS)

◆ ◆

Rice-Stuffed Squid

This is Japan's "ikameshi" (stuffed squid) Greek style.

5 tbsp	olive oil, divided	75 mL
1	onion, minced	1
8	baby squid, legs removed and chopped, bodies skinned, cleaned and washed	8
1 cup	uncooked rice	250 mL
1/4 cup	raisins	50 mL
1/4 cup	toasted pine nuts	50 mL
3 tbsp	minced fresh parsley	45 mL
1 tsp	Tabasco® garlic pepper sauce blend, divided	5 mL
	Salt and freshly ground black pepper to taste	
1/2 cup	white wine	125 mL
1 1/2 cups	tomato juice	375 mL
8	black olives, for garnish	8

◆ Heat 3 tbsp (45 mL) of olive oil in a skillet over moderate heat until hot but not smoking. Add onion and cook 4 minutes, stirring constantly.

◆ Transfer onion to a bowl and stir in squid legs, rice, raisins, pine nuts, parsley, 1/2 tsp (2 mL) Tabasco garlic pepper sauce blend, salt and pepper. Mix well.

◆ Stuff squid bodies with rice mixture and seal openings with toothpicks.

◆ Heat remaining 2 tbsp (30 mL) of olive oil over moderate heat in a large skillet. Add squid and cook 2 minutes on each side. Stir in white wine, tomato juice and remaining Tabasco garlic pepper sauce blend. Cover and cook 25 minutes, stirring occasionally.

◆ Transfer squid and sauce onto individual serving plates and garnish with olives.

(4 SERVINGS)

Add onion to hot oil and cook 4 minutes, stirring constantly.

Combine onion, squid legs, rice, raisins, pine nuts, parsley, 1/2 of Tabasco garlic pepper sauce blend, salt and pepper.

Stuff squid bodies with rice mixture and seal openings with toothpicks.

Heat remaining olive oil over moderate heat. Add squid and cook 2 minutes on each side.

Stir white wine into skillet with squid.

Add tomato juice and remaining Tabasco garlic pepper sauce blend. Cover and cook 25 minutes, stirring occasionally.

◆◆◆◆◆◆◆◆◆◆◆◆◆◆◆◆◆◆◆◆◆◆◆◆

Shrimp Tacos with Cabbage

Soft tacos with jalapeño filling.

1 lb	cooked shrimp, shelled, deveined and coarsely chopped	450 g
½ cup	chopped onion	125 mL
4 tsp	Tabasco® jalapeño sauce, divided	20 mL
½ cup	chopped pimento-stuffed green olives	125 mL
1	large tomato, seeded and diced	1
½ lb	cabbage, cored and finely chopped	225 g
½ cup	crema Mexicana (Mexican-style whipping cream)*	125 mL
3 tbsp	finely chopped cilantro	45 mL
½ tsp	salt	2 mL
12	corn tortillas, warmed	12

◆ In a medium bowl, combine shrimp, onion, 2 tsp (10 mL) Tabasco jalapeño sauce, olives and tomato. Toss to mix well.

◆ In a separate bowl, combine cabbage, crema Mexicana, cilantro, remaining 2 tsp (10 mL) Tabasco jalapeño sauce and salt. Gently toss to mix well.

◆ Place small amount of shrimp mixture in center of each tortilla; top with 2 tbsp (30 mL) prepared cabbage. Fold tortilla over filling to form taco. Repeat with remaining tortillas. Serve immediately.

* *Sour cream mixed with 2 tbsp (30 mL) milk or cream may be substituted for crema Mexicana.*

(6 SERVINGS)

Skillet-Grilled Scallops

Cook the scallops quickly in a very hot heavy skillet until they are light brown on the surface.

1 lb	medium scallops	450 g
1 tbsp	mayonnaise	15 mL
2 tsp	lemon juice	10 mL
1 tsp	Worcestershire sauce	5 mL
3 tbsp	olive oil, divided	45 mL
1 tbsp	sliced green onions	15 mL
1/4 tsp	Tabasco® pepper sauce	1 mL
1/2 tsp	salt	2 mL
1/2 tsp	freshly ground pepper	2 mL

◆ Rinse scallops well to remove sand; dry thoroughly on paper towels.

◆ In a small bowl, mix mayonnaise, lemon juice, Worcestershire sauce, 1 tbsp (15 mL) olive oil, green onions and Tabasco pepper sauce; set aside.

◆ Place a heavy skillet over high heat. When it is very hot, add remaining olive oil, and heat until oil begins to smoke. Sprinkle scallops with salt and pepper and place in skillet. Cook about 1½ minutes, turning to brown on all sides.

◆ Transfer to individual plates and serve immediately with sauce.

(4 SERVINGS)

◆◆◆◆◆◆◆◆◆◆◆◆◆◆◆◆◆◆◆◆◆◆◆◆◆

Singapore Chili Crabs

Arguably the most famous dish in Singapore.

3 lbs	blue crabs	1.4 kg
3½ tbsp	peanut oil	50 mL
10	shallots, minced	10
1 tbsp	minced ginger	15 mL
1½ tsp	minced garlic	7 mL
4	Thai chilis, minced	4
2 tbsp	Shao-Hsing wine or sherry	30 mL
2 tbsp	tapioca starch mixed with 4 tbsp (60 mL) cold water	30 mL
2	large eggs, beaten	2

SAUCE:

1¼ cups	chicken broth	300 mL
3 tbsp	Tabasco® garlic pepper sauce blend	45 mL
2 tsp	freshly squeezed lemon juice	10 mL
1 tbsp	granulated sugar	15 mL
2 tsp	mushroom soy sauce	10 mL
½ cup	ketchup	125 mL
2 tsp	Shao-Hsing wine or sherry	10 mL
¼ tsp	salt	1 mL
1 tsp	sesame oil	5 mL

◆ Place crabs in a large pot of boiling water and boil 2 minutes. Drain and let cool. Discard aprons, gills, sand sacs, mouths and mandibles. Remove top shells and set aside. Cut crabs into quarters with a cleaver or heavy knife. (If small, cut in half).

◆ Combine all sauce ingredients and set aside.

◆ Heat a wok over high heat 45 seconds, add peanut oil and coat wok using spatula. When a wisp of white smoke appears, add shallots, ginger, garlic and chilis. Stir and cook 1 minute, or until aroma is released.

◆ Add crabs and top shells, stir and cook 1 minute. Add wine and cook 1 minute. Incorporate reserved sauce and stir to coat crabs.

◆ Allow sauce to boil and stir again to coat crabs. Incorporate tapioca starch and water; add to wok. Stir until sauce thickens and begins to bubble.

◆ Make a well in center of crab mixture, pour in beaten eggs and stir well until eggs become cooked in small pieces. Transfer to a heated platter and serve.

(4 SERVINGS)

◆ *165* ◆

◆ ◆

Stir together vinegar, sugar and nam pla in a small saucepan over high heat and bring to a boil.

Stir together fish, snow peas, lime zest, egg white, remaining Tabasco garlic pepper sauce blend, salt and pepper.

Shape fish mixture into 2-inch (5-cm) balls.

Thai-Style Fried Minced Fish with Snow Peas

A lovely light dish with wonderful flavor.

3 tbsp	distilled white vinegar	45 mL
1 tbsp	granulated sugar	15 mL
1/2 tsp	nam pla (Thai fish sauce)	2 mL
1 1/2 tsp	Tabasco® garlic pepper sauce blend, divided	7 mL
	Vegetable oil for deep-frying	
1 lb	skinless, boneless, white fish, minced	450 g
10	snow peas, trimmed and cut crosswise into very thin slices	10
	Grated zest from 1/4 lime	
1	large egg white	1
	Salt and freshly ground black pepper to taste	
	Thinly sliced cucumber, for garnish	
	Chopped peanuts, for garnish	

◆ Stir together vinegar, sugar and nam pla in a small saucepan over high heat and bring to a boil. Remove from heat and stir in 1/2 tsp (2 mL) Tabasco garlic pepper sauce blend. Divide into 4 shallow ramekins for serving and set aside at room temperature.

◆ Heat vegetable oil in a wok over medium high heat to 350°F (180°C).

◆ In a bowl, stir together fish, snow peas, lime zest, egg white, remaining 1 tsp (5 mL) Tabasco garlic pepper sauce blend, salt and pepper.

◆ Shape fish mixture into 2-inch (5-cm) balls. Deep-fry fish balls, in batches if necessary, until golden brown. Drain on paper towels.

◆ Arrange fish balls and cucumber slices on 4 plates, garnish with peanuts and serve with side dish of sauce.

(4 SERVINGS)

◆◆◆◆◆◆◆◆◆◆◆◆◆◆◆◆◆◆◆◆◆◆◆◆

Salmon Cakes with Jalapeño Mayonnaise

Fresh dill and jalapeño sauce perk up the salmon.

2	cooked potatoes, peeled	2
1	14³/4-oz (437-g) can pink salmon, drained and flaked	1
1	large egg	1
1/2 cup	cracker crumbs	125 mL
1 tbsp	fresh chopped dill	15 mL
1 tbsp	Tabasco® jalapeño sauce	15 mL
1 tbsp	prepared horseradish	15 mL
3/4 tsp	salt	3 mL
1 tbsp	butter or margarine	15 mL
1 tbsp	olive oil	15 mL

JALAPEÑO MAYONNAISE:

1/3 cup	mayonnaise	75 mL
2 tsp	fresh chopped dill	10 mL
1 tsp	Tabasco® jalapeño sauce	5 mL

◆ Mash potatoes in a large bowl; add salmon, egg, 1/4 cup (50 mL) cracker crumbs, dill, Tabasco jalapeño sauce, horseradish and salt. Stir until mixture is well-combined.

◆ Shape mixture into 4 1/2-inch (1-cm) thick patties. Place remaining cracker crumbs on small plate. Dip salmon cakes in crumbs to coat well on all sides.

◆ Heat butter and olive oil in a 12-inch (30-cm) skillet over medium-high heat. Add salmon cakes and cook about 4 minutes on each side, turning once.

◆ In small bowl, blend together Jalapeño Mayonnaise ingredients and serve with salmon cakes.

(4 SERVINGS)

Shrimp Étouffée

Tender shrimp simmered in aromatic vegetables.

1/2 cup	butter or margarine	125 mL
2	medium onions, chopped	2
1 cup	chopped celery	250 mL
1 cup	chopped green onions	250 mL
2	cloves garlic, minced	2
1/2 cup	all-purpose flour	125 mL
4 cups	water	1 L
4 cups	canned tomatoes, drained	1 L
2 tbsp	lemon juice	30 mL
1 tsp	salt	5 mL
2	bay leaves	2
1/4 tsp	dried thyme	1 mL
2 lbs	shrimp, peeled and deveined	900 g
1/2 tsp	Tabasco® pepper sauce	2 mL
	Hot cooked rice	

◆ Melt butter in a large saucepot over medium heat; add onions, celery, green onions and garlic. Cook 5 minutes or until tender.

◆ Add flour and stir until well-blended. Stir in water, tomatoes, lemon juice, salt, bay leaves and thyme. Bring to a boil.

◆ Reduce heat, cover and simmer 30 minutes, stirring occasionally.

◆ Add shrimp and Tabasco pepper sauce. Simmer 5 minutes or until shrimp turns pink. Remove bay leaves and serve over rice.

(8 SERVINGS)

Red Snapper Veracruz

A popular dish in Central and South America.

2 tbsp	olive oil	30 mL
1	large green bell pepper, cut into thin strips	1
1	large yellow bell pepper, cut into thin strips	1
1	medium onion, cut in half and sliced	1
1	clove garlic, crushed	1
3½ cups	canned stewed tomatoes, coarsely chopped and undrained	875 mL
¼ cup	sliced pimento-stuffed olives	50 mL
¼ cup	Tabasco® jalapeño sauce	50 mL
2 tbsp	lime juice	30 mL
½ tsp	salt	2 mL
1 lb	red snapper*	450 g
¼ cup	chopped cilantro	50 mL
3 cups	cooked yellow rice (with saffron)	750 mL
	Cilantro sprigs for garnish	

◆ Heat oil in a 12-inch (30-cm) skillet over medium heat. Add peppers and onion and cook until tender-crisp, about 5 minutes. Add garlic and cook 2 minutes.

◆ Add tomatoes with liquid, olives, Tabasco jalapeño sauce, lime juice, salt and red snapper fillets. Bring to a boil over high heat. Reduce heat to low. Cover and simmer 5 to 10 minutes, stirring occasionally, until fish is tender. Stir in chopped cilantro.

◆ Garnish with cilantro sprigs and serve with yellow rice.

* *This recipe is also wonderful with sole or flounder fillets.*

(4 SERVINGS)

◆◆◆◆◆◆◆◆◆◆◆◆◆◆◆◆◆◆◆◆◆◆◆◆◆

Spicy Fried Bonito

Golden brown chunks with a crisp coating and zesty tomato sauce.

1 lb	**bonito***	450 g
1 tbsp	**Tabasco® garlic pepper sauce blend**	15 mL
	Salt and freshly ground black pepper to taste	
2 tsp	**whole cumin seed**	10 mL
2 tsp	**whole mustard seed**	10 mL
1 tsp	**chili powder**	5 mL
1 tsp	**oregano**	5 mL
1/3 cup	**all-purpose flour**	75 mL
3 tbsp	**olive oil**	45 mL
1	**large ripe tomato, peeled, seeded and diced**	1
1 tbsp	**minced fresh cilantro or parsley**	15 mL
2 tsp	**fresh lime juice**	10 mL
	Vegetable oil for deep-frying	
	Lemon and lime wedges	
4	**radishes, trimmed and thinly sliced**	4

◆ Cut bonito into 1½-inch (3.5-cm) pieces and place in a bowl with 1 tsp (5 mL) Tabasco garlic pepper sauce blend, salt and pepper; toss to coat.

◆ Combine cumin, mustard seed, chili powder and oregano on a plate. Place flour and olive oil on 2 separate plates.

◆ Dredge bonito with spice mixture, dip into olive oil to coat well and finally, dredge in flour, shaking off excess. Place on a rack.

◆ Combine tomato, cilantro, lime juice, remaining 2 tsp (10 mL) Tabasco garlic pepper sauce blend, salt and pepper in a small bowl.

◆ Heat oil in a wok or large skillet to 350°F (180°C). Deep-fry bonito to a light golden brown and drain on paper towels. Arrange bonito on 4 serving plates with lemon and lime wedges, spoon tomato sauce over fish and sprinkle with radishes. Serve immediately.

* *Found in Atlantic, Pacific and Mediterranean waters, bonito is of the family of tuna fish. It is generally sold in steaks and is prepared in the same way as tuna.*

(4 SERVINGS)

◆◆◆◆◆◆◆◆◆◆◆◆◆◆◆◆◆◆◆◆◆◆◆◆◆

Seafood Boil

Perfect for an informal get-together.

4 qts	water	4 L
6 oz	crab boil*	180 g
1/3 cup	salt	75 mL
1/4 cup	Tabasco® pepper sauce	50 mL
1	large lemon, cut into quarters	1
8	medium white onions, peeled	8
4	artichokes, cut in half	4
3	carrots, peeled and cut into 2-inch (5-cm) pieces	3
1½ lbs	small red potatoes	675 g
4	ears corn, each cut into 3-inch (7-cm) pieces	4
3 lbs	crawfish**	1.4 kg
1 lb	large shrimp, unpeeled	450 g
1 lb	andouille sausage or kielbasa, cut into 2-inch (5-cm) pieces	450 g

◆ In a very large saucepot with a removable wire basket, combine water, crab boil, salt, Tabasco pepper sauce and lemon. Bring to a boil.

◆ Add onions, artichokes, carrots and potatoes; bring to a boil. Reduce heat to low; cover and simmer 20 minutes or until vegetables are tender. Carefully remove vegetables.

◆ To saucepot add corn, crawfish, shrimp and sausage. Bring to a boil over high heat. Reduce heat to low; cover and simmer 5 to 8 minutes, or until crawfish is tender. Carefully remove.

◆ Arrange vegetables, seafood and sausage on large platter or place on newspaper. Serve with plenty of cold beer and French bread.

* *Crab boil is a mixture of herbs and spices used for boiling seafood. Tabasco® crab boil contains mustard seed, red pepper, bay leaves, coriander seed, dill seed, allspice, filé powder, cloves and Tabasco pepper sauce.*

** *You can substitute other shellfish for crawfish. Cook blue crabs 20 minutes, dungeness crabs 25 to 30 minutes, and lobsters 25 minutes per pound.*

(8 SERVINGS)

Bring water, crab boil, salt, Tabasco pepper sauce and lemon to a boil and add onions and artichokes.

Add carrots and potatoes; bring to a boil. Reduce heat to low; cover and simmer until vegetables are tender.

To saucepot add corn, crawfish, shrimp and sausage. Bring to a boil, cover and simmer until crawfish is tender.

175

◆ ◆

Crab Cakes

Handle with care.

2 tbsp	minced fresh parsley	30 mL
1	egg, beaten	1
3 tbsp	mayonnaise	45 mL
1½ tsp	Dijon mustard	7 mL
½ tsp	Tabasco® pepper sauce	2 mL
½ tsp	salt	2 mL
1 lb	crab meat	450 g
1 cup	fresh bread crumbs, or ½ cup (125 mL) cracker crumbs	250 mL
3 tbsp	butter	45 mL

◆ In a large mixing bowl, combine parsley, egg, mayonnaise, mustard, Tabasco pepper sauce and salt.

◆ Add crab meat and bread crumbs and stir only enough to blend. Shape mixture into 6 patties.

◆ Melt butter in a large skillet over medium-high heat. Place crab cakes in skillet and pan-fry about 3 minutes per side, or until crisp and brown. Serve.

(6 SERVINGS)

Shrimp Soup

Oysters and clams are great this way too.

¼ cup	butter or margarine	50 mL
24	shrimp, cooked	24
1 tsp	celery salt	5 mL
½ tsp	paprika	2 mL
1 tbsp	Worcestershire sauce	15 mL
4 cups	milk	1 L
½ tsp	Tabasco® pepper sauce	2 mL
4	slices of toast	4

◆ Melt butter in a 3-qt (3-L) saucepan over medium heat. Add shrimp, celery salt, paprika and Worcestershire sauce. Heat 3 minutes. Add milk and bring to a boil. Remove from heat and stir in Tabasco pepper sauce.

◆ Place toast in 4 soup bowls. Ladle soup over toast, allowing 6 shrimp per bowl, and serve.

(4 SERVINGS)

◆◆◆◆◆◆◆◆◆◆◆◆◆◆◆◆◆◆◆◆◆◆◆

Steamed Striped Bass

Classic marinated fish from Hong Kong.

1	whole striped bass, 1¹/₂ to 1³/₄ lbs (675 to 800 g), prepared*	1
2 tbsp	peanut oil	30 mL
2 tbsp	minced coriander	30 mL

MARINADE:

2 tbsp	Tabasco® garlic pepper sauce blend	30 mL
1¹/₂ tbsp	Shao-Hsing wine or sherry	25 mL
2 tbsp	soy sauce	30 mL
1¹/₂ tsp	white vinegar	7 mL
1 tsp	granulated sugar	5 mL
¹/₂ tsp	salt	2 mL
	Pinch of white pepper	
2 tbsp	fermented black beans, washed and rinsed twice	30 mL
3 tbsp	shredded ginger	45 mL

◆ Combine marinade ingredients. Place fish in a steamproof dish and brush well with marinade, inside and out. Make 3 cuts with a sharp knife on each side of fish to allow fish to steam more quickly.

◆ Boil peanut oil and reserve. (This may be done in advance. When oil boils, wisps of smoke can be seen.) It need not be hot when poured over fish.

◆ Place cake rack in a wok. Pour in 6 cups (1.5 L) of boiling water. Place dish with fish on rack. Cover wok and steam 30 minutes over high heat. Check level of water regularly. Keep boiling water at hand to replenish any lost through evaporation. Check cuts in fish skin. Fish is cooked when flesh is white and firm.

◆ When done, remove fish in dish from wok. Pour boiled peanut oil over it. Sprinkle with minced coriander and serve immediately.

* *To prepare fish, remove intestines, gills and extra fat. Clean thoroughly inside and out. Rinse and dry.*

(4 SERVINGS)

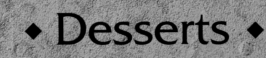

◆ Desserts ◆

Sweet and Spicy Fruitcake

Put these on your holiday gift list.

3 cups	chopped walnuts	750 mL
2 cups	chopped dried figs	500 mL
1 cup	chopped dried apricots	250 mL
1 cup	chocolate chips	250 mL
1 1/2 cups	all-purpose flour	375 mL
3/4 cup	granulated sugar	175 mL
4	large eggs	4
1/4 cup	butter or margarine, softened	50 mL
1/3 cup	apple jelly	75 mL
2 tbsp	orange-flavor liqueur	30 mL
1 tbsp	grated orange peel	15 mL
1 tbsp	vanilla extract	15 mL
2 tsp	Tabasco® pepper sauce	10 mL
1 tsp	baking powder	5 mL

◆ Preheat oven to 325°F (160°C). Grease two 3-cup (750-mL) ovenproof bowls. Line bottom and side with foil; grease foil.

◆ In a large bowl, combine walnuts, figs, apricots, chocolate chips and 1/4 cup (50 mL) flour to mix well.

◆ In a small bowl with mixer at low speed, beat sugar, eggs and butter until well-blended. Add remaining ingredients, including flour. Beat at low speed until blended. Toss mixture with dried fruit in large bowl. Spoon into prepared bowls and cover with greased foil.

◆ Bake 40 minutes; uncover and bake 40 minutes or until toothpick inserted in center comes out clean. Remove to wire racks to cool.

◆ If desired, brush cooled fruitcakes with 1 tbsp (15 mL) melted apple jelly and sprinkle each cake with 2 tbsp (30 mL) finely chopped dried apricots. Store in cool place for up to 3 weeks.

(2 SMALL FRUITCAKES)

◆ ◆

Peppery Gingerbread

Deliciously zingy!

2 cups	all-purpose flour	500 mL
1 cup	light molasses	250 mL
3/4 cup	milk	175 mL
1/2 cup	granulated sugar	125 mL
1/2 cup	butter or margarine, softened	125 mL
1 tbsp	Tabasco® pepper sauce	15 mL
1 1/2 tsp	ground ginger	7 mL
1 tsp	ground cinnamon	5 mL
1 tsp	baking soda	5 mL
1	large egg	1
	Confectioners' sugar	

◆ Preheat oven to 325°F (160°C). Grease and flour a 9 × 9-inch (22 × 22-cm) baking pan.

◆ In a large bowl with mixer at low speed, beat together all ingredients, except confectioners' sugar, until smooth. Increase speed to medium and beat 2 minutes, occasionally scraping bowl with rubber spatula.

◆ Pour batter into pan; bake 1 hour or until toothpick inserted in center comes out clean. Cool in pan on wire rack.

◆ Sprinkle top of gingerbread with confectioners' sugar.

(12 SERVINGS)

Hot Bananas with Rum and Chocolate

A surprisingly compatible combination.

4	ripe bananas	4
2 tbsp	sweet butter	30 mL
2 tbsp	dark brown sugar	30 mL
2 tbsp	honey	30 mL
3/4 tsp	Tabasco® pepper sauce	3 mL
3 tbsp	dark rum	45 mL
1 pint	vanilla ice cream	500 mL
	Chocolate flavored syrup	

◆ Peel bananas and slice into 1-inch (2.5-cm) rounds. In a large skillet, combine butter, brown sugar, honey and Tabasco pepper sauce and cook over medium-high heat until mixture sizzles. Add bananas and toss gently, until each round is coated.

◆ Raise heat to high, add rum and cook 20 seconds, or until mixture has a syrupy consistency and bananas are glazed.

◆ Scoop ice cream into 4 bowls and spoon warm bananas on top. Drizzle with chocolate sauce and serve immediately.

(4 SERVINGS)

◆◆◆◆◆◆◆◆◆◆◆◆◆◆◆◆◆◆◆◆◆◆◆

Fire and Ice Cream

This could be your new favorite dessert!

½ cup	milk	125 mL
1	medium cinnamon stick	1
1	strip orange peel	1
4	whole cloves	4
2 tsp	vanilla extract	10 mL
1	14-oz (425-mL) can sweetened condensed milk	1
1½ tsp	Tabasco® pepper sauce	7 mL
2 cups	heavy cream, whipped	500 mL
	Cinnamon sticks and orange peel twists for garnish	

◆ In a small saucepan over medium heat, combine milk, cinnamon stick, orange peel and cloves; bring to a boil. Reduce heat to low; cover and simmer 5 minutes to blend flavors. Set aside to cool to room temperature. Strain mixture.

◆ In a large bowl, combine milk mixture, vanilla extract, sweetened condensed milk and Tabasco pepper sauce. Gently fold in whipped cream. Cover and freeze until firm, stirring once.

◆ Scoop ice cream into glasses or dessert dishes. Garnish with cinnamon sticks and orange peel twists, if desired, and serve.

(6 SERVINGS)

In a small saucepan over medium heat, combine milk, cinnamon stick, orange peel and cloves; bring to a boil.

Set mixture aside to cool to room temperature and strain.

In a large bowl, combine milk mixture and vanilla extract.

Incorporate sweetened condensed milk and Tabasco pepper sauce.

Gently fold in whipped cream.

Sweet and Spicy Brownies

Deep chocolate flavor with a touch of heat.

4	squares unsweetened chocolate	4
3/4 cup	butter or margarine	175 mL
2 cups	granulated sugar	500 mL
3	large eggs	3
1 cup	all-purpose flour	250 mL
1 tbsp	Tabasco® pepper sauce	15 mL
1/2 cup	semi-sweet chocolate chips	125 mL
1/2 cup	walnuts, chopped	125 mL

◆ In a small saucepan, melt chocolate squares and butter over medium-low heat; stir frequently.

◆ Preheat oven to 350°F (180°C). Grease a 9 × 9-inch (22 × 22-cm) baking pan.

◆ In a large bowl, combine sugar, eggs, flour, Tabasco pepper sauce and melted chocolate mixture until well-blended. Stir in chocolate chips and chopped walnuts. Spoon mixture into pan.

◆ Bake 35 to 40 minutes, or until toothpick inserted in center comes out clean. Cool in pan on wire rack.

(16 BROWNIES)

Hot'n Nutty Cookies

A new taste experience.

³/4 cup	unsalted butter, softened	175 mL
1 cup	granulated sugar	250 mL
1 cup	packed brown sugar	250 mL
2 cups	peanut butter, smooth or crunchy	500 mL
¹/2 cup	macadamia nuts, chopped (optional)	125 mL
2	eggs	2
1 tsp	vanilla extract	5 mL
1 tsp	Tabasco® pepper sauce	5 mL
3 cups	all-purpose flour	750 mL
1 tsp	salt	5 mL
1 tsp	baking soda	5 mL

◆ Preheat oven to 350°F (180°C). Lightly butter and flour a cookie sheet.

◆ In a large bowl, cream together butter and sugars. Stir in peanut butter and macadamia nuts; mix until well-blended. Add eggs, vanilla and Tabasco pepper sauce. Mix well.

◆ In another bowl, mix together flour, salt and baking soda. Add to nut mixture and stir until blended.

◆ Spoon 1 heaping tbsp (15 mL) of batter per cookie onto prepared cookie sheet. Coat the tines of a fork in flour and score each cookie in a crisscross pattern. Bake 15-17 minutes, or until edges are golden. Remove cookies to rack and repeat with remaining batter.

(3 DOZEN COOKIES)

◆◆◆◆◆◆◆◆◆◆◆◆◆◆◆◆◆◆◆◆◆◆◆◆◆

Pepper Poundcake

A cake to titillate the tastebuds.

1 cup	butter or margarine	250 mL
1 cup	granulated sugar	250 mL
1 cup	firmly packed light brown sugar	250 mL
4	eggs	4
3 cups	sifted cake flour	750 mL
2 tsp	baking powder	10 mL
1/2 tsp	allspice	2 mL
1/4 tsp	salt	1 mL
1 cup	milk	250 mL
3 tsp	vanilla	15 mL
1/2 tsp	Tabasco® pepper sauce	2 mL
	Confectioners' sugar (optional)	

◆ Preheat oven to 350°F (180°C). In a medium bowl, cream butter, granulated sugar and brown sugar; beat in eggs one at a time.

◆ In a medium bowl, sift together cake flour, baking powder, allspice and salt.

◆ Alternate beating flour and milk into creamed mixture; beat in vanilla and Tabasco pepper sauce.

◇ Pour batter into lightly buttered 9-inch (22-cm) tube pan.

◆ Bake 50 to 60 minutes or until cake tester inserted in center comes out clean. Cool in pan on wire rack 20 to 30 minutes; remove from pan, and let cool completely.

◆ Dust with confectioners' sugar, if desired, and serve.

(10 SERVINGS)

Index